APPROACHING EQUALITY

EDUCATION OF THE DEAF

FRANK BOWE

Published by T. J. Publishers, Inc.
817 Silver Spring Avenue, Suite 206
Silver Spring, MD 20910

ISBN 0-93266-39-6

About the Author

Frank G. Bowe, Ph.D., LL.D., was Chairperson, Commission on Education of the Deaf [COED], 1986–1988, and editor of its Report to Congress and the President, *Toward Equality: Education of the Deaf* (1988). Dr. Bowe, a Professor, Department of Counseling, Research, Special Education and Rehabilitation [CRSR], Hofstra University, Long Island, New York, serves as Senior Editor for T.J. Publishers, Inc., for which he also wrote *Changing the Rules* (1986). He is a former Regional Commissioner, U.S. Department of Education. Other government service includes 15 years of consultation to the Congress, designation by the U.S. Secretary of State as U.S. Representative to the United Nations for planning the 1981 International Year of Disabled Persons, and membership on the U.S. House of Representatives Task Force on the Rights and Empowerment of Americans with Disabilities, the private sector group that guided Congressional consideration of the Americans with Disabilities Act, P.L. 101-336. Dr. Bowe received his B.A. degree *summa cum laude* from Western Maryland College, his M.A. in education from the Gallaudet Graduate School and his Ph.D. in educational psychology from New York University. He lives with his wife Phyllis and their daughters Doran and Whitney on Long Island's south shore.

About *Toward Equality*

"The Commission on Education of the Deaf's Report to Congress was presented at a truly historic time, when the needs of deaf education had come to the forefront. Never before has Congress commissioned this kind of broad-based study of education. As chairman of the Senate Subcommittee on Disability Policy, I have relied heavily on this report, which provides a clear and comprehensive view of the status of deaf education in this country. While many of the Commission's 52 recommendations have been addressed, I look forward to continuing to work to improve the quality and accessibility of education for adults and children with hearing impairments."

The Honorable Tom Harkin
Chairman, Subcommittee on Disability Policy
U. S. Senate

"The report of the Commission on Education of the Deaf, for example, is one of the best of its kind that I have ever seen. The Commission on Education of the Deaf report with its recommendations are as thorough, as well worked out, as clear and precise as any set of recommendations by any similar commission that I have seen, and I have seen a lot of reports by commissions."[1]

The Honorable Major R. Owens
Chairman, Subcommittee on Select Education
U. S. House of Representatives

Reference

[1]Owens, M. R. "Keynote Address". In J. E. Harkins and B. M. Virvan (Eds.) (1989) *Speech to Text: Today and Tomorrow*. Proceedings of a Conference at Gallaudet University. Washington, D.C.: Gallaudet Research Institute.

Table of Contents

Introduction

Approaching Equality is a report on implementation of the 52 recommendations presented to the Congress and the President by the Commission on Education of the Deaf [COED]. The Commission's report, *Toward Equality*, was delivered to the President, the Speaker of the House and the President pro tempore of the Senate on February 4, 1988. The 52 recommendations included 25 calling for action by the Congress, 26 for action by the U. S. Department of Education, and one for action by federally supported postsecondary programs.

What has happened in the past three years? In addressing that question, this book raises another: What remains to be done?

As of February, 1991, just three years after *Toward Equality* was issued, significant action had been taken on 26 of the 52 recommendations, or 50%. Just 6 recommendations (12%) have seen no action at all. By any measure that is a remarkable record of achievement. To what is it due?

The single most influential factor was the near-unanimity of the field in support of our report. Deaf leaders, special educators, rehabilitation counselors, interpreters, parents and virtually everyone else interested in deafness endorsed *Toward Equality*. And they kept telling Congress and the U. S. Department of Education how much they wanted its recommendations to be implemented. As just one example among many, Charles C. Estes visited the House authorizing subcommittee shortly after being appointed National Association of the Deaf [NAD] executive director in 1990. Asked what the NAD's legislative priorities were, Estes pointed to a shelved copy of *Toward Equality* and said, "That's our number one priority".

Senator Tom Harkin [D-IA], chairman of the Senate Subcommittee on Disability Policy and chairman of the Senate Labor-HHS-Education appropriations subcommittee, played a vital role in implementing the COED recommendations. The Senator and his staff—notably Robert Silverstein, Katy Beh, and Terry Muilenberg—used *Toward Equality* as a basis for lawmaking and for oversight of Executive Branch activities. Senator Harkin's letters to the Department of Education are cited throughout this report, because his persistent probing elicited much of the progress reported here. On the House side, Major R. Owens [D-NY], chairman of the House Subcommittee on Select Education, and his staff, notably Maria Cuprill and Pat Laird, were also insistent that the COED recommendations lead to legislative and executive action.

I chose the title "Approaching Equality" because I remembered the debates the 12-member Commission had in trying to decide upon a title for its final report. We rejected "Approaching Equality" at that time, in favor of "Toward Equality", because we thought the former title conveyed a more favorable state-of-the-art in deafness education than we felt was merited. The Commission was deeply distressed by what it saw in America. Now, however, three years later, considerable progress has been made. The time has come to use the title "Approaching Equality." We are getting much closer to that goal.

Legislative, executive and judicial action has occurred on 46 of COED's 52 recommendations. *Toward Equality* contributed directly to seven (7) federal laws, several Congressional resolutions and innumerable executive branch actions. In addition, at least two federal court decisions relied on *Toward Equality*. In Pennsylvania, a federal court judge found that the appropriate placement for two deaf children was a private school and not a local hearing-impaired program, because the children needed services not available locally. The Commission had stressed that federal law requires the "unique needs" of a deaf child to be met in any placement. *Visco v. District of Pittsburgh*, 684 F. Supp. 1310 (W. D. Pa. 1988). In Louisiana, COED's findings and recommendations served as a basis for a court consent decree approving placement of a profoundly deaf student at the Louisiana School for the Deaf. The consent decree stipulated that a main thrust of the COED report is the acknowledgement that for some deaf students, placement in regular classes might deny them an appropriate education that meets their unique needs. *Austin v. Clausen*, Civil Action No. 87-741 A (M. D. La. 1988).

The story of how the Commission's report generated so much activity in such a short period of time is an exciting one for anyone who cares about deaf people and about America.

It is, however, a story that inevitably reaches deep into "inside-the-Beltway" issues and problems that often baffle people who do not live and work in Washington. As an example, this book is riddled with acronyms. I've used several already; I will use a lot more. That's why a separate section presents each acronym in alphabetical order and explains what each means.

Where did COED come from? The Commission was created by title III of the Education of the Deaf Act [EDA] of 1986, PL 99-371. Section 301 of that Act states: "There is established a Commission on Education of the Deaf to make a study of the quality of infant and early childhood education programs and of elementary, secondary, post-secondary, adult and continuing education furnished to deaf individuals." Members were to be appointed by the Congress and the President. Section 302 defined the duties of the Commission. COED was given nine (9) issues to examine, notably the effectiveness of federal laws authorizing services to deaf individuals. The Commission was told to submit a report within 18 months, i.e., by February 4, 1988. That report was *Toward Equality*. Section 302(c) provided that the Commission "shall cease to exist 90 days following the submission of its final report." It did, on May 4, 1988.

The Commission was very conscious that it was the first such body in more than a generation to look at the state-of-the-art in deafness education. The earlier group had been an advisory committee appointed by the Secretary of Health, Education, and Welfare [HEW] in 1964. There's another acronym. Until 1980, HEW was the major social services agency in Washington; that year, it was split into the U.S. Department of Health and Human Services [HHS] and the U.S.

Department of Education [ED]. This advisory committee was chaired by a gentleman named Homer Babbidge. Thus, in true Washington fashion, the committee quickly became known as the "Babbidge Committee." Its report—*Education of the Deaf: A Report to the Secretary of Health, Education, and Welfare by his Advisory Committee on Education of the Deaf* (1965)—had a long, mouth-filling name. Not surprisingly, it, too, took on its chairman's name: it became known as "the Babbidge Report".

The Commission held its first meeting in January, 1988. Its last was one year later. That COED was able to do so much, so fast, is due to its members and staff. Prominent among them were: Patty Hughes, a deaf woman from Washington State, who served as chair of the Commission's executive committee; Gertrude Galloway, a deaf woman from Maryland who later became head of the Marie H. Katzenbach School for the Deaf in New Jersey, who chaired the pre-college programs committee handling pre-school, elementary, and secondary education; and William Gainer, a senior executive at the General Accounting Office (GAO), the Congressional watchdog agency, who made the Commission's leadership "coed" by chairing our post-secondary committee. All three performed admirably in difficult assignments.

Other Commission members were Dr. Gary Austin, a rehabilitation counseling professor from Illinois; Dr. Dennis Gjerdingen, a school superintendent from Massachusetts; Peter Greenough, a journalist from New York City and husband of opera star Beverly Sills; Dr. William Johnson, a school superintendent from Iowa; Dr. Henry Klopping, another school superintendent, from California; David Nelson, a Congressional aide from Washington, DC; Gary Olsen, at the time executive director of the National Association of the Deaf and later superintendent of the Mississippi School for the Deaf; and Sharon Speck, a hard-of-hearing nurse from Ohio. Together, they did their jobs so well that serving with them was a genuine pleasure. The only sad part was that Nanette Fabray MacDougall, the actress from Hollywood, had to resign shortly after we started due to family illness.

Unlike the Babbidge Committee, which included only one person who was deaf, our Commission had a deaf majority. In fact, of our 12 members, 8, or 75%, were deaf or hard-of-hearing. The chairperson, chair of the executive committee, and chair of the pre-college committee all were deaf. The two senior staff members who worked for the Commission—staff director Patricia Johanson and staff counsel Robert Mather—both were born deaf. They were ably supported by three hearing staff members—Nancy Creason, Lenore Shisler, and Suzanne Shackelford. Nancy handled our administrative work and budgets, Lenore did our post-secondary staff work, and Suzanne our pre-college staff work. In addition, Lisa Gorove interpreted and helped administer the office during COED's first several months.

As one measure of my respect for Commission members and staff, I asked them to comment on a draft version of this report. Their advice was illuminating, and I owe them a debt of gratitude for helping me to make this report accurate.

I also received comments on the draft from Dr. I. King Jordan, president of Gallaudet University; Dr. William E. Castle, director of the National Technical

Institute for the Deaf at the Rochester Institute of Technology; Charles C. Estes, executive director, National Association of the Deaf; Gerald Buckley, president, American Deafness and Rehabilitation Association; Alfred Sonnenstrahl, executive director, Telecommunications for the Deaf Inc.; Gloria Wright, head of the Office for the Deaf and Hearing Impaired, Arkansas Department of Human Services; Dr. Douglas Watson, director of the Arkansas Rehabilitation Research and Training Center on Deafness and Hearing Impairment, at the University of Arkansas, and his staff; and many others. Dr. Robert R. Davila, Assistant Secretary for Special Education and Rehabilitative Services, U.S. Department of Education, and his staff, offered information that I found very helpful and provided comments on the draft report, as did Robert Silverstein, Katy Beh and other Congressional staff members. I am grateful for their assistance. Responsibility for any errors in this report, however, is solely my own.

The kind of deaf leadership that COED exemplified was new to Washington in 1986—and it was inspiring for deaf Americans, including the students at Gallaudet. Among our draft recommendations, published in September, 1987, and sent to thousands of people throughout the nation, was that Gallaudet's leadership become like ours: comprised principally of the people it was to serve. The University at the time had only one senior leader who was deaf. One month after our Commission released its final report, the students at Gallaudet erupted in the now-famous March, 1988 "Deaf President Now" rebellion. Did COED have something to do with that? No, not really. We just set an example and proved a point that hardly needed proving—that, in words that Gallaudet President I. King Jordan later made world-famous: "Deaf people can do anything hearing people can do—except hear!"

We can—if given a chance. That chance has to begin with a good education. That's why the work reported in this book is so important: through it, America is laying the foundation for generations of young people, a foundation upon which they can stand in pride. That's why, too, the work remaining is urgently important. Especially in elementary and secondary education, little of substance happened in the past three years. Congress, the Department of Education and the States are still failing deaf children and youth. That failure will continue unless we act to assure "excellence" in deaf education—and soon.

Executive Summary

Three years after the Congress and the President received the February 4, 1988 final report of the US Congress Commission on Education of the Deaf [COED], *Toward Equality*, major progress has been made in educating Americans who are deaf. However, particularly with respect to K–12 education, much work remains.

Progress may be assessed in a number of ways. It is clear that Congress has been more active than has the U.S. Department of Education. It is clear, too, that there has been much more progress in the areas of technology and post-secondary education than there has been in elementary and secondary education.

Ratings

The 52 COED Recommendations are given, and ratings are assigned to progress on each, in *Appendix A*.

Accomplished is the rating used to indicate complete or near-complete implementation of a recommendation. If a recommendation called for action that has been mostly implemented, but for some that has yet to occur, the rating *Significantly Accomplished* is used. Taken together, the categories Accomplished and Significantly Accomplished comprise recommendations on which major progress has been made.

Partly Accomplished is the rating offered where more work remains to be done than has been performed to date, but on which some notable progress has been made. *No Action* marks those recommendations on which there has been no discernible progress.

Obviated is the rating used where events subsequent to publication of the Commission's report have rendered the recommendation outdated; in other words, an "obviated" recommendation is one on which the Commission, were it still in existence, likely would seek no action.

Progress by Designated Actors

Congress

The Commission's 52 recommendations included 25 calling for Congressional leadership. Of those, 17 (68%) have been completely or significantly implemented, most by new legislation (*Appendix B*). No action has yet occurred on five (20%) of the recommendations. On three (12%), action has been obviated, or made unnecessary by other events.

U.S. Department of Education

Half (26) of the Commission's 52 recommendations called for action by the federal Department of Education. Of those, 8 (31%) have been completely or mostly implemented and 18 (69%) have seen little or no action.

Other

One recommendation (COED #25) called for action by Gallaudet University, the National Technical Institute for the Deaf, and the four Regional Postsecondary Education Programs for the Deaf (RPEPDs)—California State University at Northridge, St. Paul Technical College, Seattle Community College, and the University of Tennessee Consortium. It has been significantly accomplished.

Progress by Category

Prevention and Early Identification [Chapter One]

Both recommendations in this category have been significantly accomplished. The Congress created the National Institute on Deafness and Other Communication Disorders [NIDCD] as we recommended. It was only the second new institute at the National Institutes of Health to be formed in 20 years. The U.S. Department of Education and the U.S. Department of Health and Human Services have made progress in early identification.

Elementary and Secondary Education [Chapters Two and Three]

Of 14 recommendations in this category, only one (7%) has seen much progress. That is COED Recommendation #3, calling upon the Department of Education to focus more resources toward English language acquisition by deaf students. Nine other recommendations (64%) in this category are rated Partly Accomplished. Four (29%) are rated No Action.

Postsecondary Education [Chapter Four]

Eight (80%) of the 10 recommendations in this category are rated Accomplished or Significantly Accomplished. No notable progress is apparent on two (20%).

Research [Chapter Five]

Of the two recommendations in this category, one is rated Partly Accomplished and one has been obviated.

Professional Standards [Chapter Six]

Four (36%) of the 11 recommendations in this category are rated Accomplished or Significantly Accomplished. No notable progress is apparent on 7 (64%).

Technology [Chapter Seven]

Nine (82%) of the 11 recommendations in this category are rated Accomplished or Significantly Accomplished. Action on the other two, both related to captioning, has been obviated by enactment of the Television Decoder Circuitry Act of 1990.

Other [Chapter Eight]

Both of the recommendations in this category are rated Significantly Accomplished. They called for action on clearinghouses and on deaf-blindness.

The book concludes with a chapter outlining further action needed to improve education of the deaf in the United States.

Notes on Terminology and Acronyms

ASL: American Sign Language

COED: Commission on Education of the Deaf

Deaf: The Commission adopted a broad definition of the term "deaf". We said in *Toward Equality* that by "deaf" we meant "all persons with hearing impairments, including those who are hard-of-hearing, those deafened later in life, those who are profoundly deaf, etc." We noted that there is a cultural definition such that Deaf persons (with the D capitalized) are individuals whose primary language is ASL and who identify themselves with Deaf Culture. Aside from our brief discussion of Deaf Culture, however, we used the broad definition. Ours was a report commissioned by Congress on education policy, for which reason we had to encompass the needs of all deaf persons.

ED: U. S. Department of Education

    OSERS: Office of Special Education and Rehabilitative Services

    NIDRR: National Institute on Disability and Rehabilitation Research

    RSA: Rehabilitation Services Administration

    OSEP: Office of Special Education Programs

EDA: Education of the Deaf Act, PL 99-371. EDA authorizes Gallaudet University and the National Technical Institute for the Deaf on five-year cycles. Originally scheduled to be reauthorized in late summer 1991, EDA will be amended by mid-1992. Federal education legislation, including EDA, may be reauthorized as much as one year later than their statutory dates due to Congressional action subsequent to the enactment of EDA in 1986.

EHA: Education of the Handicapped Act. This was until 1990 the inclusive term for federal special education legislation. PL 101-476, the Education of the Handicapped Act Amendments of 1990, changed it to the Individuals with Disabilities Education Act. Henceforth, the basic law is abbreviated as IDEA, not EHA. Accordingly, this text uses the term "IDEA" throughout, except when changing "EHA" to "IDEA" would alter quoted material or when referring specifically to provisions in PL 101-476.

FCC: Federal Communications Commission

IDEA: Individuals with Disabilities Education Act. The new name for what was previously called "EHA". See "EHA", above.

IEP: Individualized Education Program. This is the written plan prepared for every child and youth with a disability who receives special education services. The starting point in preparing an IEP is the child's "unique needs". For each such need, suitable services are identified. An "appropriate" education is one providing those services. Often, two or more programs are identified as appropriate. In that case, IDEA requires that the one which is least restrictive be selected for the child's placement.

HHS: U. S. Department of Health and Human Services.

LRE: Least Restrictive Environment. IDEA requires that, other things being equal, a child be placed in the appropriate setting most approximating that he/she would attend if not disabled.

NIDCD: National Institute on Deafness and Other Communication Disorders, in the National Institutes of Health [NIH]

RID: Registry of Interpreters for the Deaf. This is a private, not-for-profit association of sign-language and oral interpreters.

Chapter 1

Prevention and Early Identification

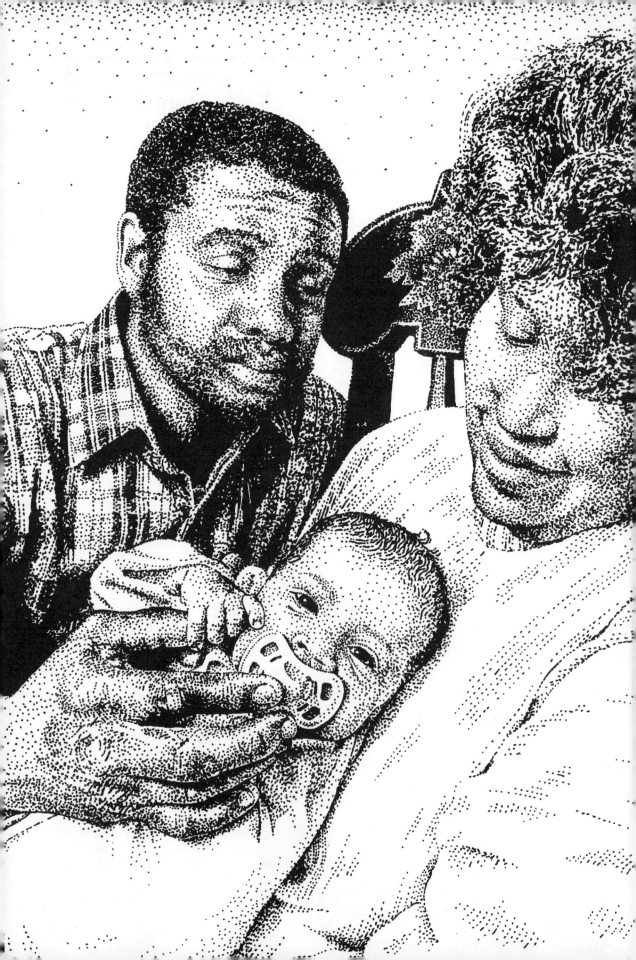

Prevention and Early Identification

Summary

The Commission adopted a chronological order for its 52 recommendations, from birth through the school years to adulthood. For this reason, the first recommendations dealt with prevention and amelioration of hearing loss. The recommendations were not presented in priority order. Some individuals, especially deaf adults concerned with deaf culture issues, objected to the first two recommendations, believing incorrectly that the Commission's perspective was one of a "medical model" of deafness. These objections overlooked the fact that in COED Recommendation #4, the Commission specifically stressed the importance of deaf culture in educating deaf children and youth and that in COED Recommendation #15, the Commission strongly recognized, and urged enhanced status for, American Sign Language [ASL].

COED Recommendations #1 and #2 have been "significantly accomplished": considerable progress has been made on each.

Prevention

COED Recommendation #1: The Congress should establish a National Institute on Deafness and Other Communication Disorders within the National Institutes of Health.

Status: Significantly Accomplished

P. L. 100-553, The National Deafness and Other Communication Disorders Act of 1988, signed by President Reagan October 28, 1988, implemented this recommendation by establishing a National Institute on Deafness and Other Communication Disorders [NIDCD].

The Commission was concerned that very little research on hearing was being funded by the Federal Government. No one Federal agency had primary responsibility for such research. Relative to the size of the population, fewer research dollars were targeted for deafness and other hearing impairments than was the case for other major disabilities. The Commission further noted that more than half of all childhood deafness is present at birth or occurs during the first year of life, and that in the vast majority of cases, both parents are hearing and usually unaware of deafness and its ramifications. One in every 22 infants is born with a hearing or other communication impairment. Disorders of hearing, speech, and language are estimated to cost the U. S. economy some $30 billion annually in lost productivity, special education and related services costs, and medical expenditures.[2] We were also concerned that much deafness arises from to-date unknown causes.

The legislation directed the Institute to study etiology, pathology, detection, treatment and prevention of hearing loss. It also consolidated in NIDCD existing National Institutes of Health [NIH] programs on balance, voice, speech, language, taste and smell, folding them into the NIDCD mission.

The NIDCD began life with a budget of $96 million, some 55%–60% of it allocated for research on deafness and hearing loss. Within three months of enactment of the legislation, January 17–19, 1989, NIDCD convened a task force of 100 scientists to prepare a "National Strategic Research Plan" to guide its work. That Plan, dated April 1989, was required by the legislation. In 352 pages, it outlined a program of basic and clinical research and for studies on use of technologies to improve the quality of life of people with communication disorders.[2]

In September, 1990 the NIDCD convened a "Working Group" to consider deaf culture, sign language, and English language development questions that the Institute could investigate. The advisory meeting was co-chaired by I. King Jordan, president of Gallaudet University, and Carol Padden, of the University of California at San Diego. The group recommended more studies such as those being conducted at The Salk Institute, in La Jolla, California, on the biological foundations of sign language acquisition, by Ursula Bellugi and her colleagues.[3]

Unmet Needs: The NIDCD budget at this writing is in excess of $120 million annually. That is more than double the amount spent each year on all disabilities by the Department of Education's National Institute on Disability and Rehabilitation Research [NIDRR]. As impressive as progress to date is, considerable work remains for advocates in deafness to sensitize the Institute's leadership to deaf-culture and sign-language-related issues.

I have seen no effort on the part of the Institute's administration to appoint deaf persons to high-level positions nor, in representative numbers, to key advisory boards.

Two kinds of actions are necessary. First, researchers in deafness need to propose state-of-the-art basic research studies in these fields to NIDCD. As is true for other NIH institutes, NIDCD funds the best applications it receives; if it receives few proposals for work important to the deaf community, it will fund few. NIDCD Director James B. Snow, Jr., M.D., told the Working Group that he welcomed more applications for basic research on issues important to the deaf community.

Second, the National Association of the Deaf and other organizations in deafness need to educate Institute leadership on deaf-community concerns. The tendency to date has been to criticize NIDCD as insensitive rather than to advocate to make the Institute more responsive to the community. Gallaudet President I. King Jordan and Self Help for Hard of Hearing People executive director Howard E. ("Rocky") Stone sit on key NIDCD advisory groups and are well-positioned to assist the NAD and other groups to channel their advocacy efforts effectively. The urgent need for both kinds of action is responsible for lowering the achievement level in COED Recommendation #1 from "Accomplished" to "Significantly Accomplished".

Early Identification

COED Recommendation #2: The Department of Education, in collaboration with the Department of Health and Human Services, should issue federal guidelines to assist states in implementing improved screening procedures for each live birth. The guidelines should include the use of high-risk criteria and should delineate subsequent follow-up procedures for infants and young children considered to be at risk for hearing impairments.

Status: Significantly Accomplished

The Commission was strong in its conviction that education and rehabilitation for persons who are deaf will be successful only if identification of hearing loss is immediate and leads promptly to early intervention. We were concerned that fewer than half of the States had in place, when our Report was published, high-risk hearing screening programs. We also noted that the average age at which hearing loss was detected in the U. S. was 2.5 years, much later than, for example, the 7–9 months reported in Israel.

The U. S. Department of Education [ED] and the U. S. Department of Health and Human Services [HHS] agreed in 1988 to sponsor a three-year study of early identification methodologies. In 1989 and 1990, about $500,000 was allocated to the study, which is looking at how auditory impairments are identified and how those techniques can be improved. The Rehabilitation Engineering Center at the Lexington Center for the Deaf, in Queens, New York, funded by the Education Department's National Institute on Disability and Rehabilitation Research [NIDRR], is exploring new technologies for identification of hearing loss in infants.[4]

Robert R. Davila, Ph.D., vice president for Pre-College Programs at Gallaudet University and deaf himself, was nominated by President Bush to become the first individual with a disability to hold the position of Assistant Secretary for Special Education and Rehabilitation Services [OSERS], U. S. Department of Education, since the position was created in 1980. On June 30, 1989, Dr. Davila told Senator Tom Harkin, chairman of the Senate Subcommittee on Disability Policy, that one of his five top policy initiatives if confirmed as Assistant Secretary would be early intervention programs. Dr. Davila has followed up by announcing priorities for early childhood research institutes funded over five-year periods to provide information that can be used by federal, state and local policymakers to improve early intervention services.[5]

NIDCD, as well, is studying early intervention techniques. Congress also acted to advance COED Recommendation #2. In PL 101-476, the Education of the Handicapped Act Amendments of 1990, Congress highlighted the importance of dissemination to parents of information about early intervention services.

Unmet Needs: Remaining to be accomplished is the development of guidelines based on these, and other, studies. COED Recommendation #2 called for ED and HHS to issue guidelines and recommendations to States. The research studies now being conducted by NIDCD and ED are expected to result in knowledge about "best practices". Because deafness is a low-incidence disability about which few early intervention specialists have expert knowledge, federal guidelines on serving deaf infants and toddlers are particularly important. Such guidelines take on additional urgency because the devastating effects on language acquisition of early childhood deafness can best be ameliorated during the very early preschool years when the brain is "primed" to learn language.

In mid-1991, Congress plans to reauthorize Part H, the section of IDEA which supports services to infants and toddlers with disabilities from birth through age two inclusive. The new Part H offers a major opportunity to implement more fully COED Recommendation #2.

Part H of IDEA contains no "least restrictive environment" provision. That is, unlike Part B [which authorizes services for children and youth aged 3–21 and which requires, in section 612(5)(B), that "to the maximum extent appropriate", children and youth with disabilities be educated with peers who are not disabled], Part H has no Congressional placement preference. Congress has signalled that it may in 1991 create a placement preference for Part H, but that this probably will be for services that keep the infant or toddler with the family—that is, services provided in the home. Thus, for deaf youngsters under three years of age, early intervention services may be offered in specially designed settings geared to meeting the full range of their needs. Services may be offered in homes, at clinics, and in day or residential schools specializing in services for deaf children. There is no need in Part H to balance the unique service needs of such children against the competing requirements of other children.

Given these opportunities to provide services young deaf children need without counterbalancing pressures, States need to learn what intervention strategies help these children. Thus, findings from studies funded by NIDCD, ED and HHS should be translated into practical strategies that state and local early intervention programs can implement. It is particularly important that long-term projects, such as ED's planned early childhood research institutes, be charged with the task of interpreting research results in practical terms that health practitioners, therapists and early childhood educators can recognize as concrete suggestions they can implement on a day-to-day basis.

References

[2]National Institute on Deafness and Other Communication Disorders. (1989) *A Report of the Task Force on the National Strategic Research Plan*. Bethesda, MD: Author.

[3]"The Working Group on Research and Training at the National Institute on Deafness and Other Communication Disorders from a Deaf Community Perspective: Report to Dr. James B. Snow, Jr., Director." Unpublished manuscript, February 1, 1991.

[4]Davila, R. R. (1989) Letter to Senator Harkin, September 25.

[5]Davila, R. R. (1989) Letter to Senator Harkin, June 30. The early childhood research institute priorities were announced in the July 31, 1990 *Federal Register*.

Chapter 2

Elementary and Secondary Education

Elementary and Secondary Education

Summary

Many of COED's recommendations on elementary and secondary education called for different interpretations of federal law or, more simply, for better communication between the Department of Education in Washington and State Education Agencies [SEAs] and Local Education Agencies [LEAs]. Although some of these recommendations were modest, implementation has been slow, as ED has resisted telling States what to do.

The Commission received more public comment about the issues related to COED Recommendations #4 and #5 than about any others. We found widespread and very deep discontent among parents, deaf students, and special educators. They complained that the law, especially Part B, was being misinterpreted and alleged that deaf children were suffering as a result. Part B authorizes services to children and youth with disabilities aged 3–21. It guarantees "appropriate" special education and related services to every child or youth with a disability. There is a Congressional preference in Part B that "to the maximum extent appropriate", children and youth with disabilities be educated with peers who are not disabled. This "least restrictive environment" language is very controversial in deaf education. In response to our recommendations, ED at first stonewalled, insisting that nothing was wrong. It was several years before the Department recognized that there were in fact serious and pervasive problems in the way it was implementing the "appropriate education" and "least restrictive environment" provisions. As this is written, ED's limited corrective actions have just begun to respond to these problems.

Making progress in this area is difficult at the federal level. Some well-intentioned advocates want to change the law itself. That, however, could lead to fewer rather than more rights. The Individuals with Disabilities Education Act [IDEA] is a carefully crafted compromise document—and Part B is a civil rights statute. To protect the rights of children and youth with disabilities, Congress is justly reluctant to "open" Part B for changes. The proper focus for change, the focus COED adopted, is the Department of Education's interpretation and implementation of the law, not the law itself. Unfortunately, ED also is severely constrained in how much it can change its regulations. Altering rules as COED requested might lead, inadvertently, to deleterious effects for other groups.

The result of all this was a careful "dance" by the Commission. In making recommendations related to implementation of IDEA, it was cautious. Some readers of *Toward Equality*, unfamiliar with the "inside-the-Beltway" cross-currents to which the Commission was responding, misunderstood this caution. Others were, and remain, baffled why some COED Recommendations which appeared on their faces to be ambitious—such as #42 that all new TV sets be equipped to receive and display captions—were rapidly implemented, while more modest COED Recommendations, such as #7 on potential harmful effects, have seen such little progress. Now they know why.

Language Acquisition

COED Recommendation #3: The Congress and the Department of Education should ensure that facilitating English language acquisition in students who are deaf (including vocal, visual, and written language) is a paramount concern guiding the implementation of exemplary practices; the establishment of program models; the dissemination of research priorities; the design of curricula, materials, and assessment instruments; and the provision of professional and parent training. Language acquisition should be a top priority in federally funded research.

Status: Significantly Accomplished

The Commission was deeply distressed by the striking lack of discernible progress in reading and other language achievement levels by deaf children over the past 20 years. Deaf children seem to reach a "plateau" at third-grade reading comprehension levels. At age 18, they receive comprehension scores comparable to those achieved by hearing students at age 8.

These third-grade reading levels were well-known to professionals in deafness education when the Commission called attention to them; they were not, however, general knowledge in America. When the author testified before the Senate Subcommittee on Disability Policy on March 21, 1988, presenting the COED Final Report, Cable News Network [CNN] and other news media focused on these third-grade reading levels as my most "news-worthy" comments.

The Office of Special Education Programs [OSEP], a unit in the Office of Special Education and Rehabilitation Services [OSERS], has funded nine (9) projects on language acquisition in deaf and hearing-impaired children since *Toward Equality* was published. The annual outlays for these projects total more than one million dollars. Many focus on use of advanced technology to teach English to deaf children. In addition, in late 1988, ED awarded a three-year grant to Rhode Island's Corliss Institute to examine English language skills of deaf children and youth. A Symposium on Language, Literacy and Deafness was held March 17–19, 1989, in Newport, RI; its *Proceedings* were published later that year.[6]

Unmet Needs: ED has devoted impressive resources to the important problem of learning how to enhance language acquisition by deaf students. Remaining now is the urgent work of applying what we learn in these studies to school curricula and materials and professional and parent training programs.

While ED has stepped up its support for research on language acquisition by deaf children, the fact remains that the field of deaf education still does not know much about how deaf children learn language. Some 175 years of effort, since Laurent Clerc began planning the curriculum for the American Asylum for the Deaf and Dumb in Hartford, Connecticut, has been remarkably unproductive:

deaf students still are graduated from high schools coast to coast with third- or fourth-grade reading achievement scores. We still don't know enough about how the brain processes visual information to be able to design educational strategies making maximum use of the sense of sight, which in most deaf children is not impaired. What we have learned is that *teaching* language to deaf children is extremely difficult and may even be impossible; we now know that they have to *learn* language. But that merely begs the question: how can we help them learn it?

These are the issues on which ED must focus, translating research findings into practical suggestions for educators and parents.

Appropriate Education

COED Recommendation #4: The Department of Education should provide guidelines and technical assistance to state and local educational agencies and parents to ensure that an individual education program for a child who is deaf takes into consideration the following: severity of hearing loss and the potential for using residual hearing; academic level and learning style; communicative needs and the preferred mode of communication; linguistic, cultural, social, and emotional needs; placement preference; individual motivation; and family support.

Status: Partly Accomplished

The Commission highlighted the importance in IDEA of "unique needs". The listing of needs in *Toward Equality*—COED spelled out linguistic, communication, social, cultural, emotional, and family needs—was intended to call national attention to the fact that such unique needs may be used to create Individualized Education Programs [IEPs] for deaf children. Since the IEP process calls for appropriate services to be provided for each such unique need, the Commission was convinced that parents who specify such needs and insist that they be included in IEPs, together with services for each, would be assuring for their deaf children the best educational services permissible under the law.

Assistant Secretary Davila, in a letter[4] to Senator Harkin, dated September 25, 1989, stated:

> "At the time the COED study was conducted, more than a decade had passed since the current legislation and accompanying policies were implemented. The findings of the Commission clearly indicate that some reevaluation of existing practices, when applied to students who are deaf, may be in order."

Shortly thereafter, OSEP convened a National Task Force on the Integration of Hearing Impaired Students to examine quality indicators and program standards for programs serving deaf and hard-of-hearing students. The final report was issued in 1990.[7] It listed basic program specifications. In an April 22, 1990 policy letter[8] [policy letters are official OSEP responses to inquiries from the public on specific issues in IDEA] to Mr. Lawrence Siegel, an attorney with the Bay Area Center for Law and the Deaf, in San Rafael, CA, OSEP released "clarifications of the Department's position" in three areas of deafness education: IEPs for deaf children, language needs of deaf students, and interpretation of the least restrictive environment [LRE] requirement. This "clarification" is as close as the Department has come to implementing COED Recommendation #4, but it suggests that more is coming.

COED Recommendation #4 sought to have ED require SEAs and LEAs to place greater emphasis on the "unique needs" of deaf children when preparing IEPs. Siegel raised "communication access" and "language needs" as unique needs, calling them "core needs". ED's response was signed by Judy A. Schrag, Ed.D., OSEP Director. She stated:

> In your discussion about peers and staff who can appropriately communicate, you indicate that '[t]he IEP is a rather technical process and document, which does not mandate a discussion of these core needs.' The purpose of the IEP is to determine how to appropriately meet the child's unique needs. We believe that consideration of each of the factors in your letter is an essential part of the IEP and placement process under the current regulations.
>
> As the examples you have given indicate, however, this does not mean that these needs are being addressed and met for all children who are deaf or hearing impaired. We are exploring what steps we can take to make sure that school districts are aware that each of the factors listed in A. of your letter is an essential part of the determination of what is a free appropriate public education (FAPE) for each child who is deaf or hearing impaired, so that these determinations will be an integral part of the IEP process.[8]

Unmet Needs: The Siegel policy letter signals a remarkable turnaround by ED. More than 30 months after COED called its attention to the urgent need to reform SEA and LEA interpretation of the law, the Department finally admitted the need for "clarification" of federal policy. The Department at long last conceded that "this does not mean these [unique] needs are being addressed and met for all children who are deaf or hearing impaired." After more than two years of stonewalling, this is a welcome softening of policy. The Siegel letter is an important one for parents and advocates to cite in their continuing battles with misinformed SEA and LEA officials. To understand the issues at hand, the author suggests that parents and advocates obtain both the January 16, 1990 letter Mr. Siegel sent to ED [from Mr. Siegel at the Bay Area Center for Law and the Deaf, 1010 B St., Suite 400, San Rafael, CA 94901; 408-298-5443] and the Department's response [request the 4/22/90 Schrag letter to Siegel by writing to: U. S. Department of Education, OSEP, 400 Maryland Ave. SW, Washington, DC 20202-2500]. Readers may also consult the *Education of the Handicapped Law Report* [16 *EHLR* 797-800, June 29, 1990].

As welcome as this "clarification" is, more remains to be done. As Dr. Schrag states, ED needs to find other avenues through which it can communicate with SEAs and LEAs to ensure compliance with the law and with the regulations. COED Recommendation #4 suggested the use of OSEP guidelines and technical assistance.

Mr. Siegel is a member of the National Association of the Deaf's National Commission on Equal Educational Opportunities for Deaf Children [NAD/NCEEODC]. The NAD's commission should not be confused with COED: the NAD/NCEEODC is a privately funded effort created by the NAD Board, while COED was a federal body created by the U. S. Congress. On behalf of the NAD/NCEEODC, Mr. Siegel drafted a "Deaf Child's Educational Bill of Rights,"[8] drawing heavily from the COED list of unique needs. It was submitted to Senators Kennedy and Harkin and to Dr. Davila early in 1991.

The 11-item "Bill of Rights" includes needs for language acquisition, communication mode, language accessibility, peer interaction, assessment/identification, support services, interpreter services, affirmative action, alternative programs, monitoring, and a special administrative unit within the U. S. Department of Education responsible for deaf education.

With few exceptions, the 11 items are within the Department's jurisdiction and as such may be implemented administratively. The major exceptions have to do with the Bilingual Education Act's definition of "limited English proficiency" [which is addressed below, under COED Recommendation #15] and personnel requirements, which are set by state and local school agencies. That the Department "may" implement much of the "Bill of Rights" is not to say that this would readily be accomplished. In particular, the NAD/NCEEODC has not established the need for a separate administrative unit on deaf education in the Department.

As discussed further under COED Recommendation #16, it is also possible that Congress may direct the federally funded "model" schools to implement these rights when it reauthorizes the Education of the Deaf Act by mid-1992. In this way, Congress would send a message to the States that they are also, by implication, to respect the rights of deaf children they serve.

Least Restrictive Environment

COED Recommendation #5: The Department of Education should refocus the least restrictive environment concept by emphasizing appropriateness over least restrictive environment.

Status: Partly Accomplished

Hearings conducted by the Commission revealed that throughout the nation, LEAs and SEAs were interpreting guidance they were receiving from the Department as saying that LRE was the cardinal principle to be followed in preparing IEPs and in placing deaf children. That LEA and SEA officials made such decisions is hardly surprising in view of the unrelenting emphasis on LRE from 1983 to 1988 by Assistant Secretary Madeleine Will, Davila's

predecessor. Illustrative are remarks Mrs. Will made on January 8, 1985, which were quoted in *Toward Equality*:

> "Education in the . . . [LRE] is what I envision as the last barrier to full implementation of Public Law 94-142. . . . In my own mind all [my beliefs] have evolved with the concept of least restrictive environment as the core concept."

The Commission's examination of PL 94-142 did not support such beliefs. LRE is not even mentioned in the Act's statement of purpose; notable in that statement, however, are the concepts of appropriate education and unique needs. One does not even reach the idea of LRE until much further into the Act; even there, the words "least restrictive environment" do not appear. What section 612(5)(B) states is: ". . . to the maximum extent appropriate, children with disabilities are educated with children who are not disabled." [Note: the original language was "handicapped children" and "who are not handicapped", but those terms were changed by PL 101-476.]

The Commission's intent was to correct what it perceived as widespread erroneous misinterpretation of the intent of the law. Recommendation #5 sought to have ED clarify the idea, obvious to the Commission, that an appropriate education was more important than was LRE. We noted that the National Council on Disability [NCD], the independent federal watchdog charged with monitoring ED and other federal agency programs, in 1986 had said the same thing that we were saying:

> Congress should direct the Department of Education to promulgate and enforce standards for the application of the least restrictive environment requirement; such standards should clarify that the primary determinant of which educational setting is the least restrictive is the educational appropriateness of the program.[9]

Both COED and NCD issued these recommendations following extensive public forums and other outreach activities designed to find out, not what Washington thought was happening, but what was really going on in SEAs and LEAs. The Council found in special education generally, and the Commission in deafness education, that "the word" around the nation varied considerably from the intent of Congress as articulated in IDEA. Both COED and NCD wanted ED to correct these misunderstandings.

Assistant Secretary Davila's September 25, 1989, letter[4] to Senator Harkin reiterated ED's position: ". . . the Department does not believe that a refocusing of concepts is needed." However, the 1990 policy letter[8] to Siegel indicates that ED is at long last beginning to understand that the Commission was right: the States are not implementing the law as well as ED had thought they were. After stating "we do not believe that regulatory changes are needed," OSEP Director Schrag concedes: "However, the Department is concerned about the questions you raise." That is a remarkable admission.

Dr. Schrag continues:

> Your letter proposes an elaboration of EHA-B's LRE requirements to address the communications needs of children who are deaf or hearing impaired. Under EHA-B, all children with handicaps, regardless of the severity of their handicap, have the right to be educated in the least restrictive educational setting in which an appropriate education can be provided. 34 CFR 300.550-300.556. Thus, public agencies are required to make available a range of placement options known as a continuum of alternative placements, including instruction in regular classes, special classes, home instruction, and instruction in hospitals and institutions. 34 CFR 300.551(a)(2). The options on this continuum must be available to the extent necessary to implement each child's IEP. 34 CFR 300.552(b) Therefore, State and local educators must take the necessary steps to ensure that qualified personnel are available in a range of placement options to meet the unique educational needs of all children with the eleven handicapping conditions recognized under EHA-B. In the case of children who are deaf or hearing impaired, it is essential that staff who can communicate in a mode of communication appropriate to children who are deaf or hearing impaired are made available in a range of placement options.[8]

Unmet Needs: The Department in the Siegel policy letter placed the emphasis upon "appropriate", and stressed that educators and other workers able to communicate with children who are deaf must be on staff in the programs on the continuum. Clearly, placement alternatives not having such staff would not qualify as "appropriate". This letter should prove very helpful to parents and advocates in eliminating placements in inappropriate settings just because school officials think those are LRE placements.

What the Department needs to do now is to ensure that "State and local educators ... take the necessary steps. . . ."

What would those steps be? The Department could explain, in clear language, that any placement being considered for a deaf child must have on staff special educators and related services personnel able to communicate with that child. For some deaf children, that will mean ASL-fluent staff members; for others, it will mean staff able to use Signed English; and for yet others, it will mean staff who speak with clear enunciation. The Department could warn SEAs and LEAs that placement into programs lacking communication-capable staff is clearly inappropriate and should not be made, no matter how "least restrictive" the setting otherwise appears to be.

Curriculum

COED Recommendation #6: The Department of Education should issue a policy statement to permit consideration in placement decisions of curriculum content and methods of curricular delivery required by the nature or severity of the child's handicapping conditions.

Status: Partly Accomplished

COED agreed with NCD[9] that "[t]he Department of Education incorrectly interprets LRE as elimininating curriculum content and method of curriculum delivery as factors to be considered in the placement of a child". We said that for many deaf children, especially those with very limited English skills, curriculum content was basic to their unique needs.

In a June 16, 1988 letter[10] to Senator Harkin, then-Assistant Secretary for OSERS Madeleine C. Will stated:

> The Department agrees that the design of each child's educational program should take into account matters of curriculum content and methods of curricular delivery. Whenever a child has special needs in these areas, they should be addressed in the child's IEP. . . . The Department does not believe that a further policy statement in this area is needed, since the Department has placed a priority for several years on encouraging schools to use a variety of methods of curricular delivery to assist children with special needs.[10]

This was responsive to the COED and NCD recommendations. However, saying that "the Department has placed a priority" on this "for several years" is inaccurate; the Department had been sending very different signals to States. As recently as 1986, its monitoring manuals[11] had proscribed use of "curriculum content or methods of curriculum delivery" in making placement decisions.

Unmet Needs: The need remains for the Department to publicize its "priority" so as to assure SEAs and LEAs that they may consider curriculum content and methods in writing IEPs. Both the Commission and the Council found widespread beliefs in the States that such considerations were improper.

At a minimum, Departmental monitoring manuals should reflect the policy articulated in the 1988 Will letter. But because the belief "out there" remains one of "there's something wrong with using curriculum content or methods of curriculum delivery as a basis for placement," the Department has an affirmative obligation to correct the misunderstandings it itself created. That means issuing, as COED recommended, a specific policy statement telling SEAs and LEAs that curriculum may in fact be a proper consideration in placement decisions. This is important because for some deaf children, notably those with very limited English skills, the most pressing unique needs may well be for intensive curricular attention to language development—and federal policy should allow, very explicitly, for schools to respond to those urgent needs.

Potential Harmful Effects

COED Recommendation #7: The Department of Education should issue guidelines and standards by which school officials and parents can, in selecting the least restrictive environment, consider potential harmful effects on the child or on the quality of services which the child needs.

Status: Partly Accomplished

The Commission noted that IDEA permits recognition of "potential harmful effects" on a child of placement in what otherwise would be the least restrictive environment. We wanted ED to emphasize that where such effects exist—we noted excessive travel time, unreasonably wide age ranges in a single classroom, and "special" classes comprised of children with very different disabilities as examples of potential harmful effects—the LEA may make a placement instead in the next more restrictive environment so as to avoid deleterious effects on a child.

Mrs. Will's June 16, 1988 letter[10] to Senator Harkin agreed that potential harmful effects must be considered in selecting the LRE, but added: "technical assistance to school officials continues to be helpful".

Unmet Needs: The Department needs to call greater attention to the potential harmful effects exception to the LRE requirement and to explain to SEAs, LEAs and parents how to apply it. It is disingenuous of the Department to say that "technical assistance to school officials continues to be helpful" when it is offering very little such guidance on ways to use the "potential harmful effects" exception to the law's LRE requirement. The Commission specifically recommended that such guidelines be issued, together with "standards"— objective criteria for determining when potential harmful effects exist.

Here, as in so many other areas connected to elementary and secondary education of children and youth with disabilities, the Department needs to take corrective action to ameliorate the effects of its earlier failure to communicate the law to SEAs and LEAs. As an example of what the Department might do, it could issue policy statements to all 16,000 school districts acknowledging that "misunderstandings have arisen about how to apply the potential harmful effects language in IDEA" ~~and~~ and stating, in clear and unambiguous terms, that the child's needs override LRE requirements where strict application of the LRE principle would harm the child.

The Department should also clarify what should be obvious: these are *potential* harmful effects. There is no need for a child actually to be harmed before the placement is changed to the next more restrictive setting.

Removal from Regular Classrooms

> **COED Recommendation #8: The Department of Education should publish in the *Federal Register* a policy interpretation that removal from the regular classroom does not require compelling evidence.**

Status: No Action

This recommendation emerged, as did so many others in this section, from hearings and other public forums. People "out there" in the States told us that SEA and LEA officials learned about an ED "Manual 10" requirement that "compelling evidence" must be demonstrated before a disabled child could be removed from a regular classroom into a more specialized setting. Manual 10 is the Department's internal monitoring guide that deals with least restrictive environment. The Commission knew that ED had withdrawn that version of "Manual 10" and replaced it with a revised edition that did not contain the "compelling evidence" standard which, in any event, had no basis in law. The hearings convinced us, however, that many educators had not recognized that ED had changed its thinking. We wanted the Department to clear things up.

The Department consistently has stated that no change is needed. They had changed "Manual 10", they said; at any rate, "Manual 10" does not apply to SEAs and LEAs, they argued, but is guidance for ED's own employees when they monitor SEA and LEA activities.

Unmet Needs: There is no legal basis for imposing a high "compelling evidence" standard for removal of a child with a disability from a regular classroom, and there never was. ED agrees.[10] But that is not how many people in the States see it. It remains important for ED to clarify all this by setting up a compelling evidence "straw man" and knocking it down. The Department should state in unequivocal terms that placement of a child into a setting, and removal from that setting, may occur on the same bases—and acknowledge that its earlier version of Manual 10 created misunderstandings. Educators of the deaf have vivid recollections of the original Manual 10—and report continuing encounters with SEA and LEA officials who are not aware of the Department's withdrawal of the "compelling evidence" standard.

References

[6]Blackwell, P. (Ed.) (1989) *Proceedings of the Corliss Institute Symposium on Language, Literacy and Deafness.* Warren, RI: Corliss. [Copies available from Peter Blackwell, Rhode Island School for the Deaf, Corliss Park, Providence, RI 02908.]

[7]*Report of the National Task Force on the Integration of Hearing Impaired Students.* (1990) Concord, NH: Parent Information Center. [Copies: PIC, P.O. Box 1422, Concord, NH 03302; 603-224-7005.]

[8]Schrag, J.A. (1990) Letter to Mr. Lawrence Siegel, April 22. Siegel's letter was sent January 16. See also 16 EHLR 797-800, supplement 268, June 29, 1990. Further information is offered in the "Deaf Child's Educational Bill of Rights" drafted by Mr. Siegel for the National Association of the Deaf's National Commission on Equal Educational Opportunities for Deaf Children [NAD/NCEEODC], January 10, 1991. Copies: NAD, 814 Thayer Avenue, Silver Spring, MD 20910; 301-587-1788.

[9]National Council on Disability. (1986) *Toward Independence: An Assessment of Federal Laws and Programs Affecting Persons with Disabilities.* Washington, DC: Author. Page 48.

[10]Will, M. C. (1988) Letter to Senator Harkin, June 16.

[11]U. S. Department of Education. (1986) *Standards and Guidelines for Compliance with Federal Requirements for the Education of the Handicapped*, p. 20.

Chapter 3

Other Elementary and Secondary Education Issues

Other Elementary and Secondary Education Issues

Center Schools

COED Recommendation #9: The Department of Education should monitor states to ensure that they maintain and nurture center schools as placement options as required by law.

Status: Partly Accomplished

IDEA requires SEAs and LEAs to maintain a full "continuum" of placement options. The reason for this is simple enough: children with disabilities differ. They differ between and within themselves: what is right for one child may not be right for another, and what is right for a child one year might not be the next year. Only by having a full range of options available can SEAs and LEAs respond to these diverse needs.

Two such options are separate day schools and separate residential schools. *Toward Equality* called these "center schools"; by that, we meant specialized programs serving children who are deaf or severely hard-of-hearing. During the 1980s, many States were closing or sharply reducing the budgets of such schools. In fact, enrollment in private residential schools for deaf children declined by two-thirds between 1974, the year before Part B was first enacted, and 1984, ten years later. The decline in public residential schools was less drastic (18% in the same ten-year period), but substantial nonetheless.

COED felt it was important that ED remind the States that such schools were part of the "continuum" and as such should be maintained and, indeed, nurtured. Residential schools today instruct about one-third of all school-age deaf children. That enrollments remain substantial despite more than a decade of concerted ED pressure against them suggests that they fill an important role in deaf education. This reinforces what COED recommended: the Department needs to preserve center schools so that they will continue to serve as viable placement options for those children who need them.

We were asking for something that we felt was fairly obvious. The law calls for a "continuum" of placement options. The 1970s-era model of a "cascade" of placements, in which some are "least restrictive" and others "most restrictive", had long since been discredited, we thought. ED itself has stated that "the overriding rule . . . is that placements are made on an individual basis."[12] How could that rule be followed if some placements were judged "least" or "most" restrictive, *a priori*, before a child's unique needs even were determined? We felt it was self-evident that they could not be. Placement options, in and of themselves, are neither "least restrictive" nor "most restrictive". They are just placement options. It is only after the unique needs have been specified, and services delineated to meet each, that appropriate placements can be identified, from which one may be selected as least restrictive.

The Department consistently claimed, for years, that no change was needed, and that no reminders for SEAs or LEAs were required. However, ED took an important step in a November 17, 1989 policy letter[13] to Robert T. Dawson, president, the Florida School for the Deaf and the Blind, in St. Augustine, FL. In this letter, Assistant Secretary Davila stated:

> Your letter asks if the interpretation under Part B of the Education of the Handicapped Act (EHA-B) . . . requires that a residential school for the deaf and the blind be included as part of a continuum of services. . . .
>
> Under 34 CFR 300.552(b), '[t]he various alternative placements included under 34 CFR 300.551 are available to the extent necessary to implement the individualized education program for each handicapped child.' Thus, if a special school is the alternative on the continuum necessary to implement a particular child's IEP, a school district would have to make this placement alternative available. In a particular case, a residential school, such as the Florida School for the Deaf and the Blind, could be selected as the placement option with the 'special school' alternative.[13]

This policy letter offers the most encouraging evidence to date that ED may monitor SEAs and LEAs to ensure that they do in fact act to ensure that such placements are available.

Unmet Needs: In its monitoring of SEA and LEA compliance with IDEA, ED must look to see that center schools remain available as placement options. As welcome as the Dawson policy letter interpretation is, SEAs and LEAs need to see it in action. In particular, it is rapidly becoming too late in many States to rescue center schools from the oblivion to which they have largely been confined by SEA and LEA mis-interpretation of the law. ED must act to preserve these schools while there still are schools to preserve.

COED Recommendation #10: The Department of Education should monitor states to ensure the availability and appropriateness of integrative programs for students in center schools.

Status: Partly Accomplished

The Commission balanced Recommendation #9, which sought to bolster the role of center schools, with #10, which asked ED to monitor more closely these schools' compliance with Part B of IDEA. COED recognized that center schools are subject to IDEA requirements, including those related to integration of activities so that deaf and other students have opportunities to study and play together. COED noted that several center schools had inaugurated "reverse mainstreaming" programs, in which they invited hearing children to participate in school-sponsored activities. We wanted to see more of these kinds of integrative programs. Mrs. Will's letter[10] to Senator Harkin said the Department would "continue to focus on this area." Little such monitoring had been performed, however, and little now is.

Unmet Needs: The Department has made no public announcement of any change in its monitoring practices or procedures with respect to this Recommendation. Once again, Mrs. Will was disingenuous in saying ED would "continue to focus on this area", given what can only be called a deafening silence from the Department on the issue. A welcome step by the Department would be a policy statement recognizing the valuable role played by center schools and acknowledging their efforts to comply with Part B of IDEA by planning "reverse integration" and other integrative activities.

Parent Rights

COED Recommendation #11: The Department of Education should issue a policy statement requiring that school personnel inform parents of all options in the continuum of alternative placements during each individualized education program conference.

Status: Partly Accomplished

The Commission stated in *Toward Equality* that parents were to be, under Part B, "equal partners" in the IEP process.[14] Public hearings and written comments from parents convinced us, as we reported in *Toward Equality*: "although parents should be treated as equal partners with school officials, the degree of parental involvement in educational placement decisions has, 'in practice, been very limited' ". [The quoted clause was from a statement presented to the Commission by the American Society for Deaf Children, a parent group.]

The Siegel policy letter[8] marks an important effort by ED to assure parents a more equal role. Dr. Schrag states:

> The Department, as a general matter, has supported and encouraged the concept of parental choice for all students. Parental choice in placement decisions is not required under EHA-B, but is permissible so long as the public agency determines that the placement selected by the parent would provide FAPE and meets all other EHA-B requirements. Therefore, it would be permissible under EHA-B for school officials to give a parent the right to select a child's placement from one or more public placements that have been determined appropriate for a child by the placement team based on applicable EHA-B requirements. The Department encourages State and local educators to explore methods for increasing parental input. . . .[8]

This 1990 policy letter clearly states that "it would be permissible"; this kind of straightforward declaration was missing in previous ED pronouncements. There is one other aspect to COED Recommendation #11, and that is the matter of advising parents about the alternatives among which they may choose.

The Commission was appalled how little parents of deaf children nationwide were being told by LEAs about their rights and in particular about available placement options. The Department of Education's position was that parents must be informed of those options only once; thereafter, it argued, parents presumably were aware of the options, so it was no longer necessary for school officials to list and explain placement options.

A Harris poll[15] conducted after our Report was issued confirmed our findings that parents were ill-informed about IDEA. Three out of every five parents (61%) contacted by the Louis Harris and Associates polling firm in 1989 reported having little or no knowledge about IDEA. Harris concluded:

> These findings strongly suggest that most parents do not know what services their children are entitled to, or how to go about obtaining these services. It is therefore likely that parents who are not aware of their rights will have a lower set of expectations for the performance of the school system.[15]

The Department's position was articulated in a 1986 policy letter.[16] In this letter, OSEP states that a school district must inform parents of placement options only when a child is first referred for special education services. This official notification is the only one the Department expects from school districts.

However, in the November, 1989 Dawson policy letter,[13] ED took a significant step further. Asserting that "there is no explicit EHA-B requirement that parents be informed of 'all placement options' on the continuum of alternative placements", Assistant Secretary Davila went on to note that parental consent was required prior to a child's initial placement:

> Such consent, which must be understood and agreed to in writing, means that the parent 'has been fully informed of all information relevant to the activity for which consent is sought. . . .' 34 CFR 300.500. Thus, under certain circumstances, school districts could describe information about the continuum of alternative placements to ensure that parents are able to give informed consent for initial placement."[13]

Assistant Secretary Davila further noted that school districts must describe alternative placements in their applications for IDEA Part B funds. [34 CFR 300.277(b). "Parents of children with handicaps may request such information from school districts," Dr. Davila concluded.[13]

Unmet Needs: The Dawson policy letter is an important step forward. Nonetheless, the Harris poll reaffirms our finding that one notification is insufficient— and that telling parents that they may request copies of school financial applications does not obviate the need to inform parents of alternative placement options available to *their* children. At each annual IEP conference, school officials should list, and explain the advantages/disadvantages of, each placement option and outline why they believe the parents should agree to the LEA-preferred option.

Evaluation

COED Recommendation #12: The Department of Education should monitor states to ensure that the evaluation and assessment of children who are deaf be

conducted by professionals knowledgeable about their unique needs and able to communicate effectively in the child's primary mode of communication.

Status: Partly Accomplished

IDEA requires that LEAs and other education agencies evaluate each child with a disability, that personnel performing such evaluations be "appropriately and adequately prepared and trained"[17], and that testing be performed in the child's native language or other mode of communication if possible.[18]

The Commission wanted to emphasize that assessing deaf children was difficult, requiring specially trained personnel to administer tests and to interpret results.

In addition, the term "native language" in IDEA is defined by referencing the Bilingual Education Act.[19] That Act regards a native language as one listed as such by the Department of Education. The Department had not, and as of this writing still has not, listed ASL as a native language. [However, see COED Recommendation #15 for ED's plans with respect to BEA and ASL.]

The Department's position consistently has been that no change is required. However, the Dawson policy letter[13] notes that Comment (2) to 34 CFR 300.9 states:

> If a person is deaf or blind, or has no written language, the mode of communication would be that normally used by the person (such as sign language, braille, or oral communication). . . . The Department believes it is critical that State and local educators address the communication needs of children whose handicapping conditions require different modes of communication, such as sign language or braille. For example, under EHA-B, testing or evaluation materials must be administered in a child's native language or other mode of communication appropriate to the child. 34 CFR 300.532(a)(1).[13]

This is as close as the Department has come, as of this writing to implementing COED Recommendation #12. The use of the word "critical" is particularly welcome, suggesting that communication mode might be examined in future OSEP monitoring activities.

Unmet Needs: Appropriate testing is so important that a vigorous effort, not just a routine one, to ensure SEA and LEA compliance is required for full implementatation of COED Recommendation #12. For deaf children who lack any meaningful grasp of the English language and for many whose first, or native, language is ASL, the requirement that testing be administered by personnel skilled in communicating with deaf children is expecially urgent. Educators specializing in deafness have recognized for years that unskilled test administrators may misdiagnose a deaf child as being retarded or even autistic.

Program Standards

COED Recommendation #13: The Department of Education should encourage states to establish program standards for deaf students requiring special schools or classes.

Status: Partly Accomplished

The Commission set forth in *Toward Equality* a minimum set of program standards it expected programs serving deaf students to meet, particularly in center schools. By "program standards", we meant such things as a curriculum that responds to special as well as academic needs, professionally trained educators, in-service teacher training programs, and the like, as well as such related services as counseling, speech and language therapy, and interpreters. We recognized that program standards were matters under SEA and LEA jurisdiction, for which reason we asked the Department to "encourage" their adoption. However, we strongly urged the Department to do so because so many SEAs and LEAs lacked standards for programs into which they placed deaf students.

One major exception to the SEA/LEA jurisdiction issue is the pair of demonstration schools housed on the Gallaudet University campus, the Kendall Demonstration Elementary School [KDES] and the Model Secondary School for the Deaf [MSSD]; these are federally funded schools and as such jurisdiction is retained by the federal government. Were the Congress to charge KDES and MSSD with meeting specific program standards, it would send a message to other schools and programs that they, too, might be expected soon to meet the same or similar standards.

The Department points to the 1990 report of a Parent Information Center task force[7] as evidence that it is encouraging SEAs and LEAs to adopt more comprehensive program standards. That report, partly funded by ED, is a helpful first step. It lists referral, evaluation, early intervention, preschool, and transition considerations. However, this report of a parent organization is unofficial. Much will depend upon whether OSEP encourages SEAs and LEAs to meet such standards. All it has done to date is to mail the report to persons requesting it.

The issue of program standards is very closely linked to those of "appropriate education" and "least restrictive environment". The Commission sought to ensure that any placement option along the continuum meet certain minimum standards. Were that to be done in a given school district, the LEA would greatly alleviate concerns about "dumping" children into public schools. OSEP Director Judy Schrag made a similar point in the Siegel policy letter[8] when she agreed that the Department had an obligation "to make sure that school districts are aware that each of the factors" [related to unique needs or program standards] "is an essential part of the determination of what is a free appropriate public education (FAPE) for each child who is deaf or hearing impaired, so that these determinations will be an integral part of the IEP process."

Unmet Needs: As implied in the Siegel letter, ED must tell SEAs and LEAs to meet unique needs and to establish minimum program standards. Meanwhile, the Education of the Deaf Act [EDA], PL 99-371, is to be reauthorized by Congress by August 4, 1992. That gives the Congress an opportunity to apply program standards to KDES and MSSD, by amending EDA's title I. A 1992–1994 demonstration of standards at the model schools could then be used by Congress to establish a basis for recommending such standards nationwide when reauthorizing IDEA, which expires September 30, 1994.

Quality Education

COED Recommendation #14: The Congress should pass a "Quality in Deaf Education" bill that would provide incentives to the states to enhance the quality of services provided to students who are deaf.

Status: No Action

Education in America swings along a pendulum—from "equity" at the one end to "excellence" at the other. Since about 1984, for example, reports such as "A Nation at Risk" have spurred State and national action to improve the quality of education. Virtually none of these initiatives has even mentioned special education. In contrast to regular education, special education has focused upon "equity" exclusively since 1975. There never has been a movement toward quality. The Commission felt that the time had come for a re-focusing of attention. After ten years of implementing landmark legislation establishing the right of every child, no matter how severely disabled, to an education of some kind, the Commission felt, it was important to look at what kind—to talk about the quality of education.

We recommended specific steps the Department of Education could take—among them, reporting on the achievement levels of students with disabilities. In its *Twelfth Annual Report to Congress on the Implementation of the Education of the Handicapped Act* (1990)[20], the Department finally did so. The data reported are appalling. The average deaf student gets "C's" in school. On a 4-point scale, the average grade is 2.6—or barely a "C+". Of all deaf students studied in the 1989 National Longitudinal Transition Study conducted by SRI International[21], three in ten (29%) were considered by their schools to be so marginal that they were exempted from state-required minimum competency tests prior to graduation. Of those taking such tests, only 61% passed the whole test. Three in every ten (29%) failed part of the test, and almost one in ten (9.2%) failed the whole test.

The other notable activity to date has been the emphasis placed by Assistant Secretary Davila on quality in special and deafness education. In his speeches, Dr. Davila stresses the importance of providing deaf and other disabled students with a good education. After years of unremitting emphasis from Washington on *where* children with disabilities are taught, it is refreshing to see senior ED officials talking about *what* they are taught and *how* they are taught.

Dr. Davila has sought input to help define what it is that we mean when we speak about "quality" in deafness education. This continues a dialogue between ED and State, local and university-based experts about how to define "excellence" in special education.

Unmet Needs: As encouraging as this progress is, no legislation has yet been introduced in the Congress. But at least a foundation is at long last being laid: people are talking about quality, as the Commission intended. Even if Congress does not enact legislation, States may do so. Already, California has strengthened its definition of the IDEA term "appropriate education" so as to provide some assurance of quality in special education in California. The California definition says an "appropriate" education is one that helps a child to meet his or her potential, consistent with the opportunities given to non-disabled children. That is crucial, because under the Supreme Court's decision in *Hendrick Hudson School District v. Rowley* (1982), IDEA's definition of "appropriate" conspicuously lacks any provision for helping a child to reach his or her potential. The Court's ruling, written by Justice Rehnquist, restricted the meaning of "appropriate" because "to require . . . the furnishing of every specialized service necessary to maximize each handicapped child's potential is, we think, further than Congress intended to go." The California definition raises the standard to as much assistance for maximizing potential as is offered to other students in the same program. The point here is that States indeed may go further than did Congress: they may impose higher standards and may in fact set goals for the provision of "quality" or "excellence" in deaf education.

Another alternative is also being debated. Some leaders in deafness are suggesting that since Congress failed even to consider quality when enacting the Individuals with Disabilities Education Act [IDEA] in 1990, it might be appropriate for advocates to suggest that the Education of the Deaf Act, PL 99-371, which is to be re-authorized in summer 1991, be used to establish a federal requirement for quality in deafness education. Roz Rosen, president of the National Association of the Deaf [NAD], has stated: "I support choice for educational placements but it must, absolutely MUST, meet standards for quality."[22] Ann Titus, of the Bicultural and Bilingual Department, Indiana School for the Deaf, notes that integrated programs under PL 94-142 rarely offer deaf children exposure to deaf adult role models, exposure to deaf culture, or education using American Sign Language as a first or native language. "Now is the time to evaluate if Deaf Education is best served under that public law. There is discussion among people now that perhaps Deaf Education should be funded under the Bilingual Act or maybe under the Deaf Education Act."[23]

A reasonable first step would be to charge the two federally funded "model" schools with demonstrating what "quality" means in deaf education. Such an amendment to EDA's title I would send a signal to the States that they, too, may someday be charged with similar obligations. However, it is unrealistic to hold out hope that deaf education might be removed from IDEA and authorized separately in EDA or in BEA. Neither Congress nor the Department would support such a move. The focus should remain on working within the framework of IDEA.

American Sign Language

COED Recommendation #15: The Department of Education should take positive action to encourage practices under the Bilingual Education Act that seek to enhance the quality of education received by limited-English-proficiency children whose native (primary) language is American Sign Language.

Status: No Action

The Bilingual Education Act [BEA] requires the Department of Education to maintain a list of "native languages" qualifying under BEA. IDEA references this list when it requires school districts to provide notifications and other communications to parents in their native languages. The Department never has placed ASL on that list. The Commission suggested that it do so.

Lawrence Siegel's letter to the Department raised this issue.

The April 1990 policy letter response[8] signed by OSEP Director Schrag marked the first official acknowledgement of progress toward implementing COED Recommendation #15:

> We note that under EHA-B, the term 'native language' has the meaning given that term by the Bilingual Education Act (BEA). 20 U.S.C. 1401 (21) . . . In response to recent inquiries, the Department was not able to find any evidence that Congress intended the BEA to serve the unique educational needs of individuals with hearing impairments who use sign language. However, OSERS officials have begun dialogue with BEA officials to re-examine the possibility of recognizing children whose language is American Sign Language (ASL) as limited-English-proficient under the current BEA. If such a determination is made and ASL is added to the BEA list of recognized languages, then the Department will move to clarify this status under the EHA-B's 'native language' definition.[8]

The Department's Office of the General Counsel has decided that ASL does not meet the three-part BEA test of a "native" language. Among other things, a native language is one used in the home; ASL is used as a primary (first) language by only the estimated 10% of parents of deaf children who themselves are deaf. For these reasons, the Department believes the BEA must be changed if ASL is to be considered a native language. BEA is up for reauthorization in 1992.

Unmet Needs: Assistant Secretary Davila made a good-faith, effective effort to implement this recommendation. However, given the position of the Department's lawyers, he appears unable to move forward without assistance from Congress. Congress could consider amending BEA. Section 7003(a)(1) recognizes three (3) categories of persons who are considered to be of "limited English proficiency":

> [A] individuals who were not born in the United States or whose native language is a language other than English;
>
> [B] individuals who come from environments where a language other than English is dominant; and
>
> [C] individuals who are American Indian and Alaska natives and who come from environments where a language other than English has had a significant impact on their level of English language proficiency. [20 USC 3283]

Americans who are deaf do not qualify under [B] except possibly native users of ASL, i.e., children of deaf parents. Congress might change [B] to include these children, or it might add a fourth category. Section 7003(a)(2) defines "native language" as "the language normally used by such individuals, or in the case of a child, the language normally used by the parents of the child." Thus, amending (a)(1) as suggested above would have the effect of including ASL users as qualifying under BEA.

Alternatively, Congress could amend IDEA section 602(a)(21) to re-define "native language" as "American Sign Language or the meaning given that term by section 7003(a)(2) of the Bilingual Education Act". This might be easier to do than would be an amendment to BEA itself. However, IDEA does not come up for reauthorization until 1994, two years after BEA is reauthorized.

Model Schools

COED Recommendation #16: The Congress should amend the Education of the Deaf Act to set certain priorities at the Kendall Demonstration Elementary School and the Model Secondary School for the Deaf, require annual reports to the Congress and the President, and require an evaluation and report every five years by the Department of Education's liaison office.

Status: No Action

KDES and MSSD are federally funded "demonstration" schools. The Commission found that they were "demonstrating" little of value to the nation's public school programs serving deaf children and youth. The Commission mailed several thousand copies of its "Notice of Inquiry" and "Notices of Draft Recommendations", soliciting public comments on the model schools. Responses from deafness educators, local education officials, parents, and others revealed little perceived value to the field as a whole from the work being done at the model schools. This notably is *not* to say that schools were not teaching their children; no one alleged that. Rather, commenters said that the model schools were not showing them how to meet their most urgent needs. That was especially true of MSSD, which served a population markedly different from that served by the average high-school program with deaf students, including state residential schools, day schools, and public high schools. We wanted MSSD in particular to change what it was doing. Instead of being a "prep school" whose principal mission, in practice if not in theory, was to funnel students into Gallaudet, we wanted MSSD to show the nation how to solve difficult problems the high schools told us they were having. For example, many educators told us they needed guidance on working with low-achieving deaf students, multiply disabled deaf youth, deaf children from non-English-speaking homes, and minority-group members who are deaf.

In its 1990 and 1991 requests for federal funding, Gallaudet has responded to the national priorities raised in COED Recommendation #16. Gallaudet characterizes its efforts to comply with this recommendation as "serious". It notes that in response to COED concerns, its Educational Resource Centers now only fund training and technical assistance efforts that focus on one or more of the COED priorities. Gallaudet also notes that MSSD has developed a program for learning disabled deaf students. Nonetheless, Gallaudet acknowledges that only 20% of

MSSD students read below the third grade level. Educators of the deaf told COED that the average graduate of their high school programs reads at the level of the average incoming MSSD student, which renders much of what MSSD does irrelevant to their schools.

Unmet Needs: It is worth emphasizing again that in COED Recommendation #16, the Commission was not stating that the two model schools were not teaching their students well. That was never alleged, either by the Commission itself or by educators and others responding to Commission requests for comments. Gallaudet officials apparently misunderstood this—and continue to misunderstand it. In a letter to the author dated Feburary 7, 1991, Gallaudet president I. King Jordan states: "Regarding COED Recommendation 16, you suggest once again that MSSD and KDES are basically ineffective and not responsive to their legislative mandate."[24] That is incorrect. What the Commission suggested, and this report reiterates, is that the goals of MSSD in particular be changed. COED believed that MSSD was doing well at what it was trying to do but that to a large extent it was trying to do the wrong things. We wanted it to be more of a "model" for the nation—doing what the field most needed it to do.

The EDA reauthorization offers us our only opportunity for several years to implement this recommendation. It is important that these schools respond to the priority needs of the nation's educators; unless they do so, the field's support for these schools will continue to erode. The priorities KDES and MSSD should meet were specified in *Toward Equality*. Congress may also want to receive input from educators of deaf children and youth, in order to obtain more timely input, since the Commission's priorities were prepared in late 1987.

References

[12]U. S. Department of Education. (1977) Comment to 34 CFR 300.552 (the Department's implementing regulation for IDEA).

[13]Davila, R. R. (1989) Letter to Mr. Robert Dawson, November 17. The letter was actually signed by Michael Vader, Acting Assistant Secretary, as Dr. Davila was on travel that day.

[14]34 CFR 300.340–300.349 (1987).

[15]Louis Harris and Associates. (1989) *The ICD Survey III: A Report Card on Special Education*. New York: Author. Page 20.

[16]*Education for the Handicapped Law Report*: Binder 1978–1987 EHA Rulings/ Policy Letters, 211:383–4 (1986).

[17]20 U.S.C. at 1413(3)

[18]20 U.S.C. at 1413(5)

[19]20 U.S.C. 3222 (1982).

[20]U. S. Department of Education. (1990) *Twelfth Annual Report to Congress on the Implementation of the Education of the Handicapped Act*. Washington, DC: Author. Pages 92, 96.

[21]Wagner, M. and D. Shaver (1989). *Educational Programs and Achievements of Secondary Special Education Students: Findings from the National Longitudinal Transition Study*. Menlo Park, CA: SRI International.

[22]Quoted in Wenokur, K. "Mainstreaming vs. Residential Schools." *Deaf USA*, November 1990, p. 10. Emphasis in original.

[23]Quoted in Wenokur, *op cit.*, pp. 4, 23.

[24]Jordan, I. K. (1991). Letter to Frank Bowe, February 7. The letter included responses Gallaudet prepared to the House and Senate as part of the 1990/1991 budget requests.

Chapter 4

Postsecondary Education

Summary

Major progress has been made on virtually all of the Commission's postsecondary education recommendations. In many cases, federally funded programs complied voluntarily with COED's recommendations, obviating the need for further legislation. And a foundation has been laid for great improvement in opportunities for non-college-bound youth and adults, the one postsecondary area in which COED found tremendous need.

Regional Programs

COED Recommendation #17: The Congress should increase funding to strengthen each Regional Postsecondary Education Program for the Deaf by providing a broader range of educational options, including vocational and technical training, 2-year junior college, and baccalaureate programs. The number of Regional Postsecondary Education Program for the Deaf should be increased to five. The additional program should be established in the southwest region of the United States to provide greater geographical coverage of the nation.

Status: Significantly Accomplished

The Commission was impressed by the opportunities provided for deaf youth and adults by the four (4) RPEPDs—California State University at Northridge [CSUN], St. Paul Technical College, Seattle Community College, and University of Tennessee Consortium. But the four programs taken together received just $2 million in annual funding—versus more than $70 million at the time for Gallaudet and NTID. COED wanted the RPEPDs to serve as regional resource centers—helping vocational, trade, junior colleges, colleges and universities within their geographical regions to serve deaf students. At the time *Toward Equality* was published, the RPEPDs had barely enough money to provide direct services to their own students, and none to support other post-secondary programs in the regions.

PL 101-476, the Education of the Handicapped Act Amendments of 1990, doubled the authorization ceiling for the RPEPDs to $4 million, and authorized outreach activities, including technical assistance to develop the "broader range" COED wanted. [Section 305(a)(3), amending section 625(a), 20 U.S.C. 1424a(a).] The Department of Education already had, in 1989, required the four RPEPDs to offer continuing education and technical assistance to other postsecondary programs in their regions, as COED had recommended. The new section became effective October 1, 1990. That was also the start of the 1991 Federal Fiscal Year. Congress appropriated the full $4 million for FY 1991.

Although a study[25] by RT-31, the Research and Training Center on Deafness and Hearing Impairment at the University of Arkansas had supported the COED contention that a fifth RPEPD was needed, and our belief that the right location for it was in Southwest U.S., a fifth program has yet to be created. IDEA authorizes $4 million, which the author believes is sufficient for four programs, but insufficient for five.

Unmet Needs: Consideration is being given in Congress to the option of authorizing the RPEPDs in the Education of the Deaf Act [EDA] rather than continuing to authorize them through IDEA. On the one hand, that would be logical: the major other post- secondary programs for deaf people, Gallaudet University and the National Technical Institute for the Deaf, both are authorized in EDA. If this is done, the RPEPDs should be designated "special institutions" for administrative purposes, as are GU and NTID. [The Helen Keller National Center for Deaf Blind Youths and Adults also should be designated a "special institution" for administrative purposes.] On the other hand, keeping the RPEPDs in IDEA avoids placing "all the eggs in one basket".

Debate continues on establishing a fifth RPEPD. On the one hand, COED and RT-31 both recommend the creation of a new RPEPD in the Southwest part of the country. On the other hand, the 1990 budget agreement between the President and the Congress requires that any new funding be accompanied by its own revenue sources. These issues may be resolved in the EDA reauthorization process by mid-1992. If a fifth program is authorized, the authorization ceiling should be lifted from $4 million to at least $5 million.

COED Recommendation #18: A 5-year funding cycle should be established for the Regional Postsecondary Education Programs for the Deaf.

Status: Accomplished

The Department of Education replaced the then-current 3-year funding cycle with a 5-year cycle in 1989, during the first RPEPD competition following publication of the Commission's report. The RPEPDs had made a compelling case to the Commission that 3-year funding cycles were counter-productive both for students and for staff.

Unmet Needs: None.

COED Recommendation #19: The Congress should authorize funds for each Regional Postsecondary Education Program for the Deaf to provide adult and continuing education programs within their respective regions and to assist other local educational institutions in providing such programs to adults who are deaf.

Status: Accomplished

The Department of Education added the recommended new activities to requirements RPEPDs must meet in the 1989 competition. Congress appropriated the funding required to allow the RPEPDs to perform these new duties without taking away from their traditional programs. They began meeting these new responsibilities in June, 1989. Congress appropriated additional monies, doubling the RPEPD funding, effective October 1, 1990.

Unmet Needs: None.

Comprehensive Rehabilitation Centers

COED Recommendation #20: The Congress should establish one comprehensive service center in each of the ten federal regions of the United States. These centers may be located in existing facilities or may be stand-alone units. The Commission further recommends that the comprehensive service centers be funded through a competitive bid process.

Status: Partly Accomplished

The Commission was deeply concerned that too many deaf youth and adults were being referred to college programs because no suitable vocational training centers were prepared to accommodate their needs. Very high drop-out rates among deaf college students were evidence of this. COED estimated the drop-out rates for deaf students at 79% at AA-degree programs and 71% at BA-degree programs. These figures suggest that many of those students never should have been placed in such programs in the first place—they needed very different services. That many, indeed perhaps most, deaf young people needed non-college training was also evident to us given a third-grade reading level average among those graduating from or leaving high schools. NTID's director William Castle and T. Alan Hurwitz assembled a post-COED task force that pressured Congress to implement this recommendation.

For Fiscal Year 1990, the Congress appropriated $900,000 to fund model rehabilitation centers[26]. The Department of Education awarded two grants, each for about $444,000. One is in Queens, New York City and the other is in Seattle, Washington. The two programs are federally funded until September, 1991.

Unmet Needs: It will be important for the two demonstration comprehensive service programs to report to the Department and to Congress prior to January, 1992, giving sufficient information so as to permit the Congress to determine whether to expand the number of such programs. The Commission was deeply concerned about the scarcity of programs for non-college-bound deaf youth and adults. Provision of two one-year demonstration grants does little to allay that concern. The Congress needs to take every advantage of the EDA re-authorization process by mid-1992 to establish a continuing program for serving this population.

There is another, more technical problem. The two "model" rehabilitation center programs are authorized only for one year. Such short-term funding is inappropriate for services to the "under-achieving" deaf population. It also obligates the U. S. Department of Education to go through a lengthy competitive award process. To illustrate that concern, it took one entire year for the Department to fund the Queens and Seattle projects. Congress needs to establish the authority for continuing services on at least a five-year basis so that quality services may be provided to this vastly under-served population.

Liaison Office

COED Recommendation #21: The Congress should amend the Education of the Handicapped Act and the Education of the Deaf Act to direct the Department of Education's liaison office to:

(1) coordinate the activities of Gallaudet University, the National Technical Institute for the Deaf, and the Regional Postsecondary Education Programs for the Deaf to ensure the quality of the programs and to avoid unnecessary duplication;

(2) review and comment on workplans relating to research, demonstration and evaluation activities, technical assistance, and development of instructional materials; and (3) assist in the preparation of budget requests.

Status: Accomplished

The Commission sought greater coordination among federally funded programs. With funds limited, it is important that duplication be avoided. The Department of Education did not wait for a Congressional directive, but immediately established a liaison office and began doing the recommended coordination. With respect to the recommendation language to "review and comment", in 1989 the author canvassed the former member of the Commission and advised the Congress and the Department that it was not necessary to impose more ED control over the programs than already existed. As far as the Commission's members are concerned, sufficient coordination is being performed.

Unmet Needs: The liaison office was created immediately after COED recommended it. However, the office lacks any legislative basis: it could be eliminated administratively at any time. For this reason, Congress should authorize the office when amending the Education of the Deaf Act by summer 1992. The office should be charged with coordinating ED-supported activities at Gallaudet, NTID, the four RPEPDs, and the Helen Keller National Center for Deaf-Blind Youths and Adults. It should also be told to coordinate the efforts of the comprehensive rehabilitation centers COED recommended be created. There is a fine line between Department of Education "coordination", which COED wanted, and Department "control", which COED did not want. The Education of the Deaf Act provides Gallaudet and NTID with authority to operate the schools. That's the way it should be.

Program Evaluations

COED Recommendation #22: The Department of Education should conduct program evaluations at Gallaudet University, the National Technical Institute for the Deaf, the Regional Postsecondary Education Programs for the Deaf,

and the proposed comprehensive service centers on a 5-year cycle, and submit a report of its evaluation with recommendations, to the authorizing committees of the Congress. The evaluation team should consist of outside experts in the field of deafness, program evaluation, education, and rehabilitation, including persons who are deaf.

Status: Partly Accomplished

The Education of the Deaf Act authorizes Gallaudet and NTID on five-year cycles. The Department of Education funds the RPEPDs, at COED's recommendation, on five-year cycles as well. Clearly, Congress and the Department need assessments at least that often, in order to determine what amendments are needed. Congress in the past asked its General Accounting Office [GAO] to perform such evaluations. GAO complied with these requests, but stated that it was unable to assess program quality because it lacked the expertise in deafness education that is required. GAO says its reports on Gallaudet, NTID and the RPEPDs are more descriptions of programs than evaluations. That is why COED asked for these assessments by experts in the field. The Congress appropriated $500,000 to the Department of Education in FY 1990 to fund an evaluation of Gallaudet University which begins implementation of Recommendation #22.

The Department kept saying it would evaluate Gallaudet and NTID. The Will June 16, 1988 letter[10] said Gallaudet's evaluation would "begin in the latter part of 1988". The Davila September 25, 1989 letter[4] spoke of a "comprehensive evaluation of Gallaudet University for 1990." That evaluation finally began in 1991. The Department also announced, during the recent competition for RPEPD program grants, that each RPEPD would be evaluated prior to the end of the 5-year cycle.

Unmet Needs: The Department has a responsibility to conduct these evaluations. The Congress itself lacks the knowledge needed to perform oversight of these programs and certainly lacks the time to do an adequate job. The GAO has admitted inability to do the job. The only independent evaluator remaining is the field itself—the experts nationwide who could come together on behalf of the Department to assess progress. That is beginning, with Gallaudet, and is needed as well with other programs. The Commission recognized that Gallaudet, NTID and the RPEPDs also were accredited by various academic bodies. We asked that the federal evaluations be planned in conjunction with accreditations so as not to unduly burden the colleges. The evidence so far is that this is being done.

Foreign Students

COED Recommendation #23: The National Technical Institute for the Deaf should be permitted to admit foreign students who are deaf. However, the number of foreign students should be limited to 10 percent of the student body at Gallaudet University and the National Technical Institute for the Deaf. Tuition should be increased to foreign students to cover 75% of the average per student costs at these two institutions.

Status: Accomplished

Gallaudet has been admitting foreign students for many years; NTID since the mid-1980s has been anxiously seeking permission to do so as well. The Commission had no problem with GU and NTID admitting foreign students. It *did* object to the use of U.S. Treasury funds to teach those students, however, particularly at a time when hundreds of thousands of American deaf youth and adults were without any federally funded post-high-school training opportunities. Our recommendation was that the schools, in essence, educate any foreign students they chose to admit without additional American financial resources to do so.

The Congress agreed. The report of the House-Senate conference committee on Labor-HHS-Education Appropriations [Report 101-274] for FY 1990[25] stated (p. 39):

> The conferees direct the Secretary to grant the approval for the National Technical Institute for the Deaf to admit foreign students and that such students should pay a 50-percent tuition surcharge. The conferees intend this foreign student surcharge be the same 50-percent rate for Gallaudet University and Howard University. Finally, the conferees also agree that NTID, Gallaudet University, and Howard University should have the opportunity to phase in the surcharge over a 3-year period.[26]

Gallaudet's Board of Trustees voted in 1989 to impose a 50% surcharge beginning Fall 1990, even before the Conference Committee completed its work. This action restored the rate in effect 1983–1987. [Beginning Fall 1987, Gallaudet had cut the surcharge to 20%, much to the Commission's irritation.] The effect of a percentage differential surcharge is largely what COED had recommended— the foreign students, or their home governments, would pay the bulk of the cost of their education.

Unmet Needs: The planned 3-year implementations need to be carried out. The intent is that American taxpayer levies not be used, inappropriately, to subsidize the education of students whose families are not assessed American taxes. The Commission's concern that the urgent needs of American deaf individuals not ready for college be met is also important to remember: we must meet American needs before we direct our generosity to deaf persons elsewhere on the globe.

Hearing Students at Gallaudet

COED Recommendation #24: The Congress should deny Gallaudet the latitude to accept hearing students to its baccalaureate programs.

Status: Accomplished

The Commission was concerned that the integrity of federal funding for Gallaudet might be placed at risk were it to continue aggressively to seek to admit hearing undergraduate students, as it had been doing under President Jerry C.

Lee. The Department of Education agreed. The Will letter[10] to Senator Harkin stated:

> Admission policies are the responsibility of the Board of Trustees. However, the Department takes the position that the annual Federal appropriation should not be used to subsidize the education and related costs of undergraduate students who have normal hearing, other than those enrolled in the interpreter training program."[10]

Soon after I. King Jordan's ascendance to the Presidency one month after the COED Final Report was issued, the tenor changed. President Jordan told the author he had no problems complying with the intent of COED Recommendation #24.[27] There was no need for Congress to act.

Unmet Needs: None.

Affirmative Action

COED Recommendation #25: Gallaudet University, the National Technical Institute for the Deaf, and the Regional Postsecondary Education Programs for the Deaf should continue to strengthen the positive efforts they have already made in recruiting, hiring, and promoting qualified applicants and employees who are deaf.

Status: Significantly Accomplished

When the Commission released its report, only 25% of Gallaudet's faculty and staff, and just 12% at NTID, were deaf. We noted that, for purposes of comparison, 87% of faculty and staff at Howard University, a federally supported postsecondary institution primarily for blacks, were black; similarly, at Wellesley College, a women's school, 74% of employees were women.

We were particularly troubled that the executive positions at Gallaudet and NTID were virtually all filled by hearing people. After our Report was issued in February, 1988, this became one of the rallying points in the "Deaf President Now" movement at Gallaudet. That movement, in turn, changed things greatly. As an indication of how far things have moved, the 1990 selection of a provost at Gallaudet was made from five candidates, all deaf. According to NTID Director William Castle, deaf people now comprise 15.54% of NTID employees.[28]

Unmet Needs: For many reasons, not the least of which is responsiveness to the explicit and implicit needs of deaf people, both programs should continue vigorously to recruit and hire into leadership and faculty positions persons who are deaf. This is much more than simply a matter of providing deaf students with role models. Deaf leadership of major, federally funded programs speaks volumes about the integrity of these programs. Were the leadership all-hearing, as it was in past years, the implicit message would have continued to be one of "we teach deaf people, but we don't teach them well enough to trust them with important responsibilities." At Gallaudet in particular, but in other post-secondary programs as well, the message increasingly is that qualified deaf people are in fact available in sufficient numbers that there just is no question any more than "deaf people can do anything hearing people can do—except hear."

COED Recommendation #26: The Congress should amend the Education of the Deaf Act to require that a majority of the members of the governing and advisory bodies of Gallaudet University, the National Technical Institute for the Deaf, and the Regional Postsecondary Education Programs for the Deaf be persons who are deaf.

Status: Significantly Accomplished

The Gallaudet Board of Trustees voted in October, 1988, to fill Board seats with deaf persons "as vacancies arise". Gallaudet President Jordan and NTID Director William Castle both have told the author they expect to have deaf or hard-of-hearing Board majorities by mid-1991. Jordan added that "I am personally committed to making substantial progress toward this goal."[27] Gallaudet Board of Trustees Chairman Philip Bravin noted that as of February 1991 the Gallaudet Board already had 50% membership that was deaf or hard-of-hearing, if one disregarded the ex officio Congressional members.[27] NTID Director Castle reported[28] that as of Fall 1991, 56% of the voting members of NTID's National Advisory Group will be deaf. As NAG chairman, Albert T. Pimentel, who is deaf, automatically becomes a member of the Board of Trustees of Rochester Institute of Technology [RIT], NTID's host institution. The leaders of the RPEPDs have expressed similar commitments with respect to their advisory bodies.

Unmet Needs: The programs should continue to work toward the goal expressed in COED Recommendation #26, but the need for federal legislation has been largely eliminated. The Commission hoped that its recommendation would lead to voluntary compliance so that legislation would not be required. This appears in fact to have happened.

References

[25]Watson, D. (1990) A Research-Based Proposal for a Federal Postsecondary Program to Serve Deaf Students in the Southwest and Rocky Mountain States. Unpublished report submitted January 12 to Richard K. Johnson, U. S. Department of Education. [Copies: Arkansas Rehabilitation Research and Training Center on Deafness and Hearing Impairment, University of Arkansas, 4601 W. Markham Street, Little Rock, AR 72205; 501-686-9695 (v/TDD).]

[26]House Report 101-274, Departments of Labor, Health and Human Services, and Education and Related Agencies Appropriations Bill, HR 2990, October 9, 1989, pp. 38 (comprehensive centers) and 39 (foreign students at NTID and Gallaudet).

[27]Personal communication, I. King Jordan, January 25, 1989 and Philip Bravin, February 8, 1991.

[28]Personal communication, William E. Castle, February 17, 1989 and February 1, 1991.

Summary

Both Gallaudet University and the National Technical Institute for the Deaf at Rochester Institute of Technology have performed important research over the years. The Commission's interest in their research programs was primarily managerial in nature. We sought to endorse administrative changes first suggested by the Congressional General Accounting Office (GAO), in the belief that those modifications would strengthen the programs.

Stimulating Greater Competition

COED Recommendation #27: The Congress should establish a National Center on Deafness Research within Gallaudet University. Present funding at Gallaudet University for research-related purposes would not necessarily be increased, but would be managed by the Center. A significant portion of the Center's research funds should be awarded competitively to other qualified research organizations.

Status: Obviated

The Commission's concerns in making this Recommendation were several. Some were related to Gallaudet and some to the Department of Education. Events since *Toward Equality* appeared have largely eliminated the need for the National Center.

First, we were disturbed that GAO was unable, despite repeated efforts, to identify what happened to "national mission" funds at Gallaudet's Pre-College Programs, KDES and MSSD, particularly to funds intended to support research projects and programs. Both "model" schools have two roles to play: first, to educate students in the classroom, and second, to provide technical assistance to other educational programs across the nation; the latter role is called the "national mission" function. The General Accounting Office also found that KDES and MSSD lacked management controls over research projects. GAO recommended a number of management reforms, which we endorsed.

Second, we noted that some exciting research was being performed by researchers not affiliated with Gallaudet nor with NTID. At a time that both Gallaudet and NTID received generous, stable federal support for research, researchers elsewhere competed for scarce, short-term discretionary project funds. It was our contention that the best research should be supported, regardless of where it occurred, and that free and open competition was likely to produce that effect.

There were some inside-the-Beltway political concerns, as well. The Commission was not pleased with OSERS's track record in supporting deafness-related

research. The Members expressed concern that OSERS might be tempted re-
direct monies intended for deafness-related studies toward non-deafness priorities of greater interest to OSERS political appointees. That was why the proposed
National Center was to be located at Gallaudet.

Since 1988, OSERS support for competitive grants in deafness has increased
markedly. The conditions spurring COED Recommendation #27 have changed.
The author canvassed the former members of the Commission and, on the basis
of their responses, advised the Assistant Secretary for OSERS and the Congress
that establishing a National Center at Gallaudet no longer was a priority.

Unmet Needs: Continued vigilance is necessary to assure that the changes in
OSERS are not ephemeral. Establishing a permanent, legislative basis for the
OSERS liaison office [see COED Recommendation #21, above] is one way to do
this. At the same time, public support for research at Gallaudet, particularly in
Pre-College Programs, is best assured by clear and understandable communication from Gallaudet about how the funds are being used. Research at the precol-
lege level at Gallaudet is intended to serve a national audience. That audience
most likely will support such research if it feels it has a say in setting research
priorities.

Public Comment

**COED Recommendation #28: The Congress should direct Gallaudet Univer-
sity and the National Technical Institute for the Deaf to develop concrete
research plans and to provide them for public comment by consumers and
researchers. The projects then should be selected in conjunction with a program review process involving (principally) the best researchers in the field.**

Status: Partly Accomplished

This recommendation, too, represented an endorsement by the Commission of
suggestions made by GAO. Public support for research at these institutions is
most likely to be sustained when research plans respond to national priorities
and to state-of-the-art research issues. The Commission wanted both Gallaudet
and NTID to give nationally recognized experts, as well as consumer representatives, greater opportunities to offer input into research goals and objectives.

In his September 25, 1989 letter to Senator Harkin, Assistant Secretary Davila
stated:

> [A] greater degree of coordination is desirable. Therefore, I will direct
> the National Institute on Disability and Rehabilitation Research
> (NIDRR) to reactivate its InterAgency Sub-Committee on Deafness
> Research and establish a joint NIDCD-NIDRR chair for this committee.
> Both Gallaudet University and NTID will be expected to discuss pro-
> posed research activities with Federal representatives through this
> mechanism.[4]

Although much remains to be done, Gallaudet and NTID have been noticeably more active in reaching out to consumer organizations and to prominent researchers off-campus since publication of *Toward Equality*.

Unmet Needs: Both Gallaudet and NTID are authorized by EDA. The EDA re-authorization by mid-1992 gives Congress a chance to decide how it wishes to provide more direction in this area. The Congress can insert COED Recommendation #28 almost verbatim into titles I and II of the Education Act when the Act is reauthorized. Once again, Congress can also further implemention of the COED recommendations by establishing a legislative basis for the OSERS liaison office. Dr. Davila has structured a role for that office in reviewing Gallaudet and NTID research plans, and a permanent authorization for the office will continue this exemplary practice despite changes in the Administration following presidential elections.

Professional Standards and Training

Professional Standards and Training

Summary

The Commission was convinced that improvements in education and rehabilitation for deaf persons would come only when qualified personnel in direct-services jobs (teachers, counselors, interpreters) were plentiful. Tremendous shortages in all of these fields existed when *Toward Equality* was released. Implementation of COED personnel-related recommendations has been slow in most areas, because the Department of Education insists that it is not authorized to do much with respect to personnel standards and training. The Department has not, however, sought such authority from the Congress. In that light, its passivity appears increasingly irresponsible.

Infants and Toddlers

COED Recommendation #29: The Department of Education should require state educational agencies to conduct statewide planning and implementation activities that specifically address the educational and psychological needs of families with young children who are deaf. Individuals working with young deaf children and their families should be professionally trained in the area of deafness and early intervention.

Status: Partly Accomplished

This recommendation addresses Part H of IDEA. Part H authorizes family and social services for infants and toddlers, aged birth to two inclusive. Like Part B [which authorizes special education and related services for children and youth aged 3–21], Part H is mandatory: the States must provide the services to all eligible children. PL 101-476, the 1990 Amendments, did little with Part H, except to make some technical amendments, to add social work services to the list of services to which infants and toddlers birth to age two inclusive were entitled, and to improve information dissemination to parents. Congress is reauthorizing Part H in 1991.

Part H requires the Department to provide technical assistance to States. Such help is particularly needed with respect to deaf children. Deafness is a communication disability. Everything the Commission learned about language acquisition in deaf children pointed to the irreplaceable early-childhood years: language either is learned during these early years or it is likely never mastered at all. We wanted the Department, in its technical assistance role, to call to the attention of the States the crucial importance of addressing the communication needs of deaf children virtually from the day of diagnosis.

In response to COED Recommendation #29, the Department says it intends to bring the issue of inclusion of deafness-related measures in statewide planning and implementation activities to the attention of lead agencies in the States as part of that technical assistance program. The Department also has said it agrees that early intervention personnel should be professionally trained, including in work with deaf infants and youth. However, the Department says it is limited in its ability to do what this recommendation calls for, noting that the details of statewide plans and the professional standards personnel must meet are State concerns on which the Department can only advise.

Unmet Needs: The Department has shown in this response, as in many others, that it is unwilling to tell States what to do. Congress has an opportunity in 1991 to decide if it wants to adopt deafness-specific requirements as part of statewide planning and personnel mandates. This opportunity arises as Congress re-authorizes Part H. Guidance is needed not only because deafness is a low-incidence, poorly understood disability but also because such State standards as do exist vary so widely as to indicate that many States, if not most, are in need of Departmental assistance in setting personnel and program standards.

COED Recommendation #30: The Department of Education should suggest that at least one member appointed to each State Interagency Coordinating Council be knowledgeable about deafness.

Status: Partly Accomplished

IDEA Part H requires States participating in the infants and toddlers program to assemble these Councils and requires that parents, providers, and other key groups be represented on these Councils. The Councils play an important role in Part H: the federal statute requires that services from a wide range of state and local agencies, including social, health, and family services as well as some medical assistance be provided to each eligible infant or child. Forging interagency coordination is not an easy task. The Councils provide a neutral meeting ground at which coordination plans may be made.

Dr. Davila's September 25, 1989 letter to Senator Harkin reiterated the Department's belief that it does not have the legal authority to implement this recommendation, and said:

> The Department believes that this recommendation should be brought to the attention of the appropriate State officials who determine appointments to the State Interagency Coordinating Councils.[4]

That is what the Commission recommended: that language "should suggest" means to bring to State attention the need for at least one Council member to be knowledgeable about deafness.

Unmet Needs: The Department needs to suggest that States make knowledge about deafness one of the factors used in selecting Council members. Monitoring by the Department should include collection of data showing how many States comply with the intent of this recommendation. Such information will assist the Congress in determining if further requirements for Council membership should be enacted.

COED Recommendation #31: The Department of Education should ensure that grants for personnel training be targeted to personnel providing special services, preschool, and early intervention services to deaf children, from birth to age 5, and their families. Training should also be provided to adults who are deaf to prepare them to work as facilitating team members in local intervention programs.

Status: Partly Accomplished

The Commission discovered, as have others examining special education,[9,15] that personnel training programs are just now beginning to prepare early intervention personnel knowledgeable about disabilities, including deafness. The Commission believed the issue was particularly pressing in deafness: deaf persons working in special education usually are found in secondary-level programs, rarely in preschool programs. We thought it was especially urgent that parents and early-intervention personnel bring deaf adults into Part H programs so that parent and child alike would benefit from interaction with "role models" who themselves were deaf.

The Will June 16, 1988 letter[10] to Senator Harkin noted that parents, including those who are handicapped, could be trained through Parent Training and Information programs under Part D of IDEA. Part D provides federal funds for training special education and related personnel, as well as parents. That answer misses our point: we sought to include adults who were deaf as role models and instructional aides; Mrs. Will thought we were talking about deaf parents of school-age children. Exposing deaf children to deaf adults is of proven value in assisting the children to develop realistic career and lifestyle goals.

The 1990 EHA Amendments change section 631(a)(2)(A), in Part D, to add a need for personnel to serve limited-English-proficient children. Shortages of such personnel are among the priorities to be considered in making awards for personnel preparation.

Unmet Needs: Personnel, including deaf adults, trained specifically to provide early-intervention services to families with deaf children are urgently needed. The Department needs to make this a priority for its personnel training programs. To date, the Department has not done so. Training of adults with disabilities to serve as role models and as consultants to educational programs serving deaf children is a major unmet need.

Personnel Training and Standards

COED Recommendation #32: The Department of Education should provide guidelines for states to include in their state plans such policies and procedures at least as stringent as those set by the Council on Education of the Deaf, to ensure that professionals in educational programs for students who are deaf are adequately prepared and trained.

Status: Partly Accomplished.

The Council on Education of the Deaf [CED] has established widely accepted standards for professionals in the field. Serving on CED are reprsentatives from the Alexander Graham Bell Association for the Deaf, the Convention of American Instructors of the Deaf, and the Conference of Educational Administrators Serving the Deaf. CED's standards require that teachers have skills in evaluating the needs of deaf children and in meeting those needs at the preschool, elementary, secondary and vocational education levels of instruction.

The Department points to the 1990 parent task force report[11] in responding to this recommendation. The report lists competencies for personnel, including teachers, interpreters, and related services personnel [pp. 52–77]. This unofficial report does not, however, substitute for Departmental guidelines. As noted earlier, the Department merely mails the report to persons requesting it, or tells requestors to contact the Parent Information Center in New Hampshire for copies. COED had in mind much more vigorous Departmental efforts to ensure that SEAs and LEAs employed personnel qualified to work with deaf students.

Unmet Needs: The Department needs to become more assertive about insisting upon quality in the States. It needs to advocate on behalf of the children. That is particularly urgent in States now lagging in special education efforts. In justifying its passivity, the Department says:

> The Department's understanding . . . is that Congress intended the Department to play an important role in supporting personnel development in the States, but to play a relatively limited role in the setting of particular standards for particular job categories.[10]

COED Recommendation #33: The Department of Education should require states to ensure that persons employed to teach in special education programs demonstrate competence in the instructional practices and communication methods utilized within those programs.

Status: No Action

The Department justifies its inaction on COED Recommendation #33 as it does with respect to #32: that it has a "limited role" to play under the law. The need for communication skills competence is particularly critical: studies indicate that many teachers of deaf children, whether employed in regular or special programs, lack needed communication competencies.[29]

Unmet Needs: Few things can be more basic than that teachers and related services personnel be able to communicate with children in the schools. The Department has a heavy obligation to insist that this fundamental requirement be met.

COED Recommendation #34: The Department of Education should require states to ensure that regular classroom teachers serving students who are deaf in their classes receive the necessary technical assistance and training to meet the special educational needs of the students.

Status: No Action

From 1983 to 1988, the Department of Education used every means at its disposal to push States to place deaf children into regular public schools. Each of its *Annual Reports to Congress* trumpeted the rising percentages of such children States reported serving in regular school buildings. The 1990 *Twelfth Annual*[20], for example, reported that for the 1987–1988 school year, 80.5% of deaf and hard of hearing children aged 6–21 were served in regular school buildings:

All Placements	100.0%
Regular Class	24.4
Resource Room	20.9
Separate Class	35.2
Separate School	10.8
Residential School	8.6
Home/Hospital	0.1

Research by Woodward, Allen and Schildroth[29] shows that as many as 91% of hearing teachers of deaf children in mainstreamed settings do not have appropriate communication skills. An investigation of LRE issues in deafness by Gallaudet's Donald Moores[30] offers similarly discouraging news about the competencies of regular educators and related services personnel.

Unmet Needs: Despite ED's insistence that SEAs and LEAs place deaf children in public classrooms, not one of its three reports sent to Senator Harkin on progress in implementing COED recommendations mentioned even one initiative to prepare the regular educators who were teaching these children.[4,10,31]

Bluntly, the Department's unrelenting pressure for placement in the LRE was not accompanied by any corresponding pressure on SEAs and LEAs to be sure that local schools could teach these children. The result was—and continues to be—a travesty.

COED Recommendation #35: The Congress should re-establish federal support for teacher preparation, including the recruitment of highly qualified applicants, in the field of education of the deaf. Priority for fellowships to qualified applicants should be awarded to members of minority groups and persons who are deaf.

Status: Accomplished

The 1990 EHA Amendments require, in amended section 631(a)(3) of Part D, that "priority consideration in the selection of qualified recipients of fellowships and traineeships" be given to "individuals from disadvantaged backgrounds, including minorities and individuals with disabilities who are underrepresented in the teaching profession or in the specializations in which they are being trained." States are to include in their state plans how they will "recruit, prepare and retain qualified personnel, including personnel from minority backgrounds, and personnel with disabilities." (Section 613(a)(3)). The need for minority-group educators is urgent. About one-third of deaf students but less than a tenth of their teachers are members of minority groups.

The Department of Education funded 93 projects in Fiscal Year 1990 to train deaf educators. In 1989, 224 graduates trained to work with deaf children, 80 with hard-of-hearing children, and 21 with deaf-blind children were grant-supported.

Unmet Needs: The Department's 1990 Twelfth Annual Report[20] said the States reported needing 610 more teachers of deaf and hard-of-hearing children to fill existing vacancies. Especially needed are black, Hispanic, and other minority-group educators.

Interpreters

COED Recommendation #36: The Department of Education, in consultation with consumers, professionals, and organizations, should provide guidelines for states to include in their state plans such policies and procedures for the establishment and maintenance of standards to ensure that interpreters in educational settings are adequately prepared, trained, and evaluated.

Status: Significantly Accomplished

The Commission was distressed to observe in the States an utter lack of standards for educational interpreters. Persons who could barely sign were being employed by school districts to serve as interpreters; interpreters were being assigned tutorial and other duties directly contradictory to their responsibilities under the Registry of Interpreters for the Deaf [RID] "Code of Ethics". In many schools, interpreters are paid as teacher aides, far less than they could earn elsewhere as free-lance interpreters. The better interpreters thus shun the schools.

Congress appropriated $1 million in additional personnel training monies for Fiscal Year 1990, of which the Department allocated $600,000 to interpreter training programs. Two new programs were established, including one at Northwestern Connecticut Community College [NCCC] for a program specializing in educational interpreting. The Department told NCCC that it was expected to provide technical assistance to States on standards for educational interpreters.

PL 101-476, the 1990 EHA Amendments, requires, in section 613(a)(3), that states develop a system for determining annually the number and type of personnel employed in special education and related services, including those who do not hold appropriate State certification or licensure. Such reports will assist Congress in determining the need for educational interpreters.

In 1989, with the approval of the Assistant Secretary for Special Education and Rehabilitative Services, an NTID-sponsored task force of experts on educational interpreting developed the manual *Educational Interpreting for Deaf Students*[32] which offers States guidelines for using interpreters in the classroom. The sponsors of the task force included the Registry of Interpreters for the Deaf and the

Conference of Interpreter Trainers as well as the National Association of the Deaf, the American Society for Deaf Children, the Alexander Graham Bell Association for the Deaf, the Convention of American Instructors of the Deaf and the Conference of Educational Administrators Serving the Deaf.

The NTID publication, unlike the 1990 Parent Information Center report on education program standards,[7] carries an introductory letter by Assistant Secretary Davila. That letter, on Department letterhead, states: "I encourage school administrators, teachers, interpreters, and others in local school districts to review the report and carefully consider its recommendations in developing quality educational interpreting for students who are deaf." This is the kind of Departmental support that is needed.

Unmet Needs: The issue is of sufficient importance that the Department itself should provide guidance to States, rather than relying on private organizations to do so. The 1989 manual is, nontheless, an excellent point of reference for the Department to use in telling States what they should do to ensure that SEAs and LEAs make proper use of educational interpreters.

COED Recommendation #37: The Congress should provide funding to develop training programs, design curricula, and award stipends to recruit and train potential and working educational interpreters.

Status: Accomplished

The Congress provided an additional $1 million for interpreter training in Fiscal Year 1991. The Department plans to hold competition for awards specific to educational interpreters during 1991, using these new funds. Added to the $600,000 allocated in 1990, this doubles annual outlays for interpreter training from the $900,000 in Fiscal Year 1989.

As noted above, NCCC is expected to offer technical assistance to States in using educational interpreters.

Unmet Needs: Continued funding should be provided until the desperate shortages are alleviated nationwide. The need for such assistance was magnified greatly in July 1990 when President Bush signed the Americans with Disabilities Act, PL 101-336, into law. ADA's requirements that employers and places of public accommodation provide interpreter services to deaf persons, as needed, greatly expands the demands placed on America's limited supply of qualified interpreters.

COED Recommendation #38: The Congress should fund section 315 of the Rehabilitation Act. The Department of Education should establish standards for interpreters in the field of rehabilitation and other human services settings.

Status: Partly Accomplished

The additional $600,000 allocated in Fiscal Year 1990 for interpreting was used, in part, to fund a national center specializing in rehabilitation interpreting. This program, located at the University of Tennessee at Knoxville, was told by the Department to provide technical assistance to States on how interpreters should be used in rehabilitation settings.

Unmet Needs: The Rehabilitation Act, PL 93-112 as amended, is up for re-authorization by mid-1992. The Congress has an opportunity there to consider what to do with section 315. The section authorizes grants to States to establish interpreter services programs and also authorizes the Commissioner of the Reha-bilitation Services Administration (RSA) to establish standards for interpreters in such services. It has never been funded, for which reason the RSA Commissioner never has issued such standards. Perhaps the Tennessee prorgram will develop standards for the Commissioner to review and, if appropriate, issue for use by State rehabilitation agencies. Again, enactment of ADA greatly increases the nationwide need for more interpreter training programs and for interpreter services standards.

Rehabilitation Training

COED Recommendation #39: The Department of Education should provide an increased number of traineeships for trainees specializing in deafness.

Status: Accomplished

The Department increased funding for deafness rehabilitation training by 66% between 1988 and 1990, to $1.4 million. It also increased allocations for training educational personnel to work with deaf and hard-of-hearing persons to $4.5 million in 1989 and again to $8.0 million in 1990. The 1990-over-1989 funding alone represented a 56% increase.

Unmet Needs: The 1990 levels will need to be increased further and sustained for several years before the major shortages in education and rehabilitation of deaf persons are resolved. Still, this kind of responsiveness to COED recommen-dations is very welcome. The single most urgent need in deafness rehabilitation is for specialists in work with the "under-achieving" population that requires the kinds of services that the COED-recommended comprehensive rehabilitation centers provide. These specialists must be ASL-fluent, both in expressive and in receptive skills. They must be knowledgeable about labor-market trends. And they must be trained in supported work techniques, because supported employ-ment undoubtedly will be needed by many "under-achieving" deaf individuals when they first begin performing competitive jobs.

References

[29]Woodward, J., T. Allen, and A. Schildroth. (1985) "Teachers and Deaf Stu-dents: An Ethnography of Classroom Communication." In Delaney, S., and R. Tomlin (Eds.) *Proceedings of the First Annual Pacific Linguistics Conference*. Eugene, OR: University of Oregon Press, pp. 479–493.

[30]Moores, D. F. (1991) Dissemination of a Model to Create Least Restrictive Environments for Deaf Students. Unpublished final report, # G008720128. Copies: NIDRR, US Department of Education, 330 C Street SW, Washington, DC 20202; or Dr. Moores, Center for Studies in Education and Human Development, Gallaudet University, 800 Florida Avenue NE, Washington, DC 20002.

[31]Will, M. C. (1989) Letter to Senator Harkin, January 5.

[32]Stuckless, E. R., J. C. Avery, and T. A. Hurwitz (Eds.) (1989) *Educational Interpreting for Deaf Students: Report of the National Task Force on Educational Interpreting*. Rochester, NY: NTID at Rochester Institute of Technology.

Technology

Summary

Remarkable progress has been made on the COED technology-related recommendations. Senator Harkin's personal leadership on captioning triggered full implementation of COED Recommendation #42 much more rapidly than anyone could have predicted. His commitment, along with that of Sen. Daniel K. Inouye [D-HI]; Rep. Edward J. Markey [D-MA], chairman of the Telecommunications and Finance Subcommittee in the House; and Rep. Major R. Owens [D-NY], chairman of the Select Education Subcommittee in the House, triggered other important initiatives, notably in providing funds to States for acquisition of technological aids for deaf persons and for individuals with disabilities.

Captioned TV

Toward Equality stated: "TV is the most pervasive and influential means of sharing information in America." We wanted to promote captioning. The central thrust of our argument was that this technology must become accessible to deaf persons just as existing laws required that airports, schools, libraries and other buildings be accessible to persons using wheelchairs.

We noted that caption decoders were, at the time, owned primarily by born-deaf or early deafened persons and their families. "Closed" captions are made "open" by decoding technologies. It was necessary to purchase a special decoder box and related cables, at a cost of some $180. Such "special" equipment was perceived by many senior citizens as "stigmatizing", for which reason few older persons with declining hearing bought them. Of all Americans with a hearing loss, some two-thirds are over the age of 60. The very nature of captioning—that it required purchase of a special add-on peripheral that was seen by most hearing-impaired persons as stigmatizing—would therefore constrain market growth to a small fraction of its potential.

The Commission noted, too, that captions could provide important benefits for persons who are not hearing-impaired. Captions could, for example, help preschool children learn to read. They could help illiterate adults become literate. They could help foreign-language speaking Americans acquire English. And they could help persons in other nations to learn English.

At the time we issued *Toward Equality*, just one-third of all American network television programming was captioned. And both network and caption industry testimony to the Commission warned that even that small proportion was endangered. Said ABC: "Increased decoder ownership—not just more captioning—is required for a strong, self-sustaining captioning service." The National Captioning Institute [NCI] concurred: "[T]o make the captioned service economically viable and self-sustaining, captioning must reach into at least 500,000 homes and ideally 1,000,000 homes by 1990." As of December, 1987 just 150,000 American homes had caption decoders. Industry consensus was that there was no way the number would more than triple in three years without some major stimulus. If the "critical mass" of one-half million homes were not reached soon, we were told, network and corporate sponsorship of captioning might wither away—putting captioning on a downward spiral from which it might not recover.

Our major Recommendation [#42] was that Congress act to require that virtually all new TV sets sold in America be equipped to receive and display closed captions. Such caption-ready TV sets would be, the Commission argued, the electronic equivalents of building ramps and elevators.

We envisioned computer chips built into virtually all new TV sets. Such chips were not then being manufactured. The Commission received extensive testimony, however, that they could be made—and probably would become available within a year of the emergence of demand for them.

The potential of such chips struck us as compelling. Some 15 to 20 million TV sets are sold in America each year. Thus, within one year of the introduction of caption-ready TV sets, the number of American homes capable of receiving captions would increase from a small fraction of one million to well over 15 million. A market of that size would, we believed, virtually guarantee that captioning would survive and, indeed, thrive. Every dollar spent encoding captions for TV programming would deliver a vastly greater return on investment. And just as mothers pushing baby strollers, delivery persons using dollies, bicycle riders and others discovered the benefits of curb cuts once those were widely installed in the nation's streets, so too would families discover uses for captioning.

We were convinced that a sea change in national policy was not only required to rescue the captioning industry but imperative to enable the technology to reach its intended audience. In a bold move, the Commission voted to recommend such a change in national captioning policy. To reinforce our message—that we wanted the nation to move away from the limited decoder box approach and toward built-in accessibility—we recommended that Congress immediately stop providing funds to subsidize decoder equipment.

However, the Commission was skeptical how rapidly Congress would act to require a major industry to implement our recommendation. Among the stumbling blocks: some 90% of TV sets sold in America are not made in this country, but in Japan and Korea. These kinds of international economic issues might slow or even prevent action on COED Recommendation #42. In addition, the chip upon which #42 was based did not exist when *Toward Equality* was published. So we made two other caption-related recommendations. Both were intended as interim measures—steps to enhance captioning until #42 became reality.

COED Recommendation #40: The Congress should require the Federal Communications Commission to issue regulations as it deems necessary to require that broadcasters and cable-TV programmers caption their programming.

Status: Obviated

COED Recommendation #40, that Congress require broadcasters to caption their programming, was intended as an intermediate measure. Once most American homes were caption-equipped, market forces would assure that most if not all programs were captioned, and such a requirement to caption would be unnecessary. Both broadcast and cable television are regulated industries that must conform to FCC regulations. We believed it was justifiable for our national government to use its regulatory power to promote such a social good, at least until the market took over.

Enactment of PL 101-431, the Television Decoder Circuitry Act of 1990, obviates the need for Congress to implement this recommendation. Since broadcasters, cablecasters and others in the television industry know that by mid-1993 virtually every TV set sold and/or manufactured in the U. S. will be caption-ready, the existence of a massive market will vastly increase caption activity.

Unmet Needs: None. In the unlikely event that captioning does not become widespread by the mid-1990s, further legislation or regulation may be necessary. At this time, however, no action is required.

COED Recommendation #41: The Congress should establish a Corporation of Closed Captioning to coordinate the distribution of federal funds for captioning projects. The Corporation would neither perform captioning services, nor compete for funds with captioners.

Status: Obviated

The second interim recommendation, that a Corporation of Closed Captioning be created that would distribute federal dollars subsidizing the preparation of captions for television programming, we intended to stimulate competition in captioning. We received testimony, plus voluminous written filings, alleging that the current mechanism was not working. The Department of Education at the time often funded 100% of the cost of captioning some programs. Whoever won the contract would be able to approach broadcast and cable companies with a free service, thus undercutting the other seven captioning vendors. Even if the Department were to pay only part of the cost, the contract winner still would enjoy unfair market advantages over competitors. We sought to establish a more sensible policy that would give all vendors incentive to compete, thus fostering private investment in captioning. The Commission also believed that if COED Recommendation #42 were to be implemented, the fact that tens of millions of American homes were caption-capable would reduce or even eliminate altogether the need for further federal funding for captioning. So COED Recommendation #41 was intended to serve an interim purpose.

Unmet Needs: None. Monitoring of private-sector investments in captioning may be called for in order to determine whether continued federal funding for captioning is necessary.

COED Recommendation #42: The Congress should require the Federal Communications Commission to issue rules as it deems reasonable and necessary to make new TV sets capable of decoding closed captions. Until such TV sets

**become widely available, federal funds for decoder development and manufac-
turing should be made available to increase the distribution of existing
decoders, including provision of free decoders to persons who are deaf.**

Status: Accomplished

PL 101-431, the Television Decoder Circuitry Act of 1990, requires all TV sets
13" or larger (measured diagonally) that are sold and/or made in the U. S. to be
caption-chip-equipped no later than July 1, 1993. The bill became law October
16, 1990.

The speed with which Congress acted to adopt COED Recommendation #42
was stunning. Senator Tom Harkin, chairman of the Subcommittee on Disability
Policy, announced at an appropriations hearing May 5, 1989, that he would
personally take the lead in seeing that this recommendation was implemented.
He later asked the author to discuss COED Recommendation #42 with the major
TV manufacturers, to see if they would oppose legislation requiring them to
place decoder chips into their sets. Consultations in September, 1989, with such
manufacturers as Sony, Sanyo, SamSung and others resulted in industry consensus that it would not oppose such legislation.[33,34] Senator Harkin then immediately introduced S. 1974, the Television Decoder Circuitry Act on November 21,
1989. It passed the Senate the night of August 2, 1990 by unanimous consent.

In the House, Reps. Edward J. Markey of Massachusetts and Major R. Owens of
New York introduced H.R. 4267, the House version of the bill on March 14,
1990. Mr. Markey was Chairman, Subcommittee on Telecommunications and
Finance, and Mr. Owens Chairman, Subcommittee on Select Education, in the
House. It passed the House on October 1, 1990.

President Bush signed the measure into law on October 16, 1990. It became PL
101-431. The rapid enactment of the Television Decoder Circuitry Act was
due, in part, to the lack of industry opposition. Only the Electronic Industries
Association [EIA], a trade lobbyist, opposed the bill, arguing that it would raise
consumer costs.

Even EIA came on board in July 1990. In a letter[35] to Senators Harkin and
Inouye, Gary J. Shapiro, EIA group vice president, "pledge[d] to you the Electronic Industries Association's support in working toward final passage of the
bill." The major change made at EIA's request was delay in the implementation
date from October 1, 1992 to July 1, 1993. Rapid implementation also was due
to the work of Sy DuBow, Esq., of the National Center for Law and the Deaf
[NCLD]. Mr. DuBow was tireless in his efforts to secure broad support for the
legislation. Even before the House bill was introduced, 11 TV industry groups,
9 education associations, and 37 disability organizations had told Congress they
supported the legislation.

Congress had acted earlier[36] to forbid the U. S. Department of Education from
using any federal funds to subsidize manufacturing or sale of stand-alone decoder
boxes. House Report 101-172 stated: "The Committee has not included 1990
funds to continue the subsidy for production of television decoders for the

hearing impaired." Rather than rechannel those monies toward distribution of free decoders, as COED had recommended, the Committee stated: "The Committee believes that these funds should be redirected towards the development of new technologies for the same population."[36]

Unmet Needs: None. The legislation effectively implemented the recommendation. The Federal Communications Commission, as required by the law, issued proposed regulations early in 1991.

Meanwhile, industry action was rapid. Zenith indicated that it hoped to have caption-ready TV sets on the market well before the July, 1993 deadline. Said Zenith VP Bruce Huber: "There is a whole new market out there."[37] Sanyo, Thomson and ITT were reported developing chips as early as 1990.[37]

Accessibility

COED Recommendation #43: Federal proceedings and meetings should be communicatively accessible for people who are deaf through captioning, assistive listening devices, and interpreters (when needed and arranged for in advance).

Status: Significantly Accomplished

Section 504 of the Rehabilitation Act of 1973 [PL 93-112], as amended, already required that federally conducted activities (those of federal agencies themselves) and federally supported activities (those of federal grant recipients) be accessible to and usable by persons with disabilities, including deaf people. The Commission found, however, that compliance with this requirement was sporadic.

In October, 1989, the Senate Labor and Human Resources Committee installed an assistive listening system [ALS] in its Committee Hearing Room. The system was requested in July, 1989, by Senator Harkin and was approved by Senator Kennedy, the Committee Chairman. According to *Roll Call*, a newspaper covering Capitol Hill, "It is the first time in the history of the Senate that any committee has used such a system."[38]

Use of real-time captioning in federal meetings has increased notably since *Toward Equality* appeared. The Commission set an example by using such technologies in all of its public meetings and hearings.

Unmet Needs: Although the law is clear, continued monitoring is required to ensure that compliance continues. Making meetings and other proceedings communicatively accessible often is a continuing, rather than a one-time capital, expense and thus at times may be sacrificed due to budgetary constraints.

COED Recommendation #44: Instructional materials financed and/or disseminated by the federal government, including materials for public viewing and employment training, should have open captions.

Status: Significantly Accomplished

Section 504 already requires this, but compliance has been uneven. New legislation enacted since the publication of *Toward Equality* has reinforced the message that federally financed videos and films must be captioned.

PL 101-336, the Americans with Disabilities Act of 1990, section 402 in Title IV, amends section 711 of the Communications Act of 1934: "Any television public service announcement that is produced or funded in whole or in part by any agency or instrumentality of Federal government shall include closed captioning of the verbal content of such announcement."

PL 101-476, the EHA Amendments of 1990, requires in section 661(b)(2), in Part G, that the Secretary of Education "make efforts to ensure that such [new technology and media] instructional materials are closed captioned".

The Department of Education referred this Recommendation to the Interagency Coordinating Council for section 504, of which it, the U. S. Department of Justice, and other federal agencies are members. On June 20, 1990, the ICC adopted the policy statement, "Making Government Documents and Audio-Visual Presentations Available in Accessible Formats". That policy statement urged federal agencies to caption films and videos and to make printed documents available to blind persons in accessible media, such as Braille, ASCII disks, or large print.

The Commission deliberately used the word "open" to refer to the captioning that is needed for videotapes and films that are not intended for broadcast on television. It makes no sense to close caption a training tape or film; that imposes upon trainers and meeting organizers the burden of setting up captioning equipment in the training room. Open captions, by contrast, may be viewed on any TV set. However, since PL 101-431 will eventually result in virtually all TV sets being caption-ready, the oversight is one with short-term consequences, however deleterious.

Unmet Needs: None, other than monitoring for compliance.

COED Recommendation #45: The Congress should caption its own televised proceedings, including House and Senate floor activity.

Status: Significantly Accomplished

In Fiscal Year 1990, the Secretary of the Senate provided funds to the U. S. Department of Education to support development of a request for proposals [RFP] for the purpose of soliciting bids from captioners to caption Senate floor activity broadcasts on C-SPAN. The Department issued that RFP in 1990. Captioning is to begin by mid-1991. The House announced while this book was in preparation that C-SPAN coverage of its gavel-to-gavel proceedings would be captioned beginning February 19, 1991.

Unmet Needs: None, other than monitoring for compliance.

COED Recommendation #46: The Congress should provide funds for research, development, acquisition, and maintenance of technology to be used for persons who are deaf.

Status: Accomplished

The Commission noted that the state-of-the-art in assistive technology for persons who are deaf or hearing-impaired was such that major advances in quality of life were feasible. Yet knowledge about, and ownership of, such aids among deaf persons was, we believed, very low. We were sufficiently concerned about the general lack of knowledge that we included in *Toward Equality* a five-page description of such technologies.

PL 100-407, the Technology-Related Assistance for Individuals with Disabilities Act of 1988, signed by President Reagan on August 19, implemented this recommendation by authorizing grants to States of up to $1.5 million per year for acquisition and maintenance of technological aids for persons with disabilities, including deaf people. The Act, popularly called "TRAIDA", also authorized program development projects and research on funding assistive technologies. Most States have received such title I grants.

PL 101-476, the EHA Amendments of 1990, authorizes increased use of assistive technology services and devices in the education of infants, toddlers, children and youth (section 661). The Act specifically authorizes use of federal funds for acquisition, and training in use, of assistive technologies. It also says funds may not be awarded unless the applicant agrees to coordinate activities with the State agency receiving TRAIDA title I State grant funds.

In addition, under the authority provided by title II of the Rehabilitation Act, as amended, NIDRR supports research and development projects and programs on a new generation of hearing aids, tactile aids, and speech/language training technologies for persons with hearing and speech impairments. Many States also offer Specialized Customer Premises Equipment [SCPE] distribution programs, which offer free or reduced-cost devices assisting deaf persons to use the telephone, such as TDDs, ring signallers, etc. Together, these State programs have distributed more than 40,000 TDDs and 35,000 ring signallers to deaf and hearing-impaired persons.

Unmet Needs: Sufficient legislative authority exists on the federal level to implement this recommendation. Continued progress, particularly in alerting deaf and hearing-impaired persons to what modern technology can do for them, and helping them to finance such aids, will be needed.

COED Recommendation #47: Federally funded school systems should specify accessibility of electronic equipment to persons with disabilities when such equipment is procured, leased, or rented for faculty, staff, or students.

Status: Significantly Accomplished

PL 100-407, the Technology-Related Assistance for Individuals with Disabilities Act of 1988, requires all States receiving TRAIDA grants to comply with the equipment accessibility requirements of section 508 of the Rehabilitation Act as amended in 1986 [PL 99-506]. Section 508 originally applied only to federal agencies. It requires that any electronic office equipment purchased, leased, or rented by federal agencies for use by their employees be accessible to and usable by, or adaptable for use by, persons with disabilities. TRAIDA extended these requirements to States receiving title I grants. Section 103(c)(7) requires "[a]n assurance that the State will comply with guidelines established under section 508 of the Rehabilitation Act of 1973." The obligation applies to State agencies, their units, and contractors doing business with State agencies, including State departments of education. Applicable regulations were published by the U. S. Department of Education on August 9, 1989.

As noted earlier, PL 101-476, the EHA Amendments of 1990, authorizes funds for assistive devices and services for children and youth. The obligation in the Act for coordination with the TRAIDA agency should spur compliance with section 508.

Unmet Needs: The Department of Education should ensure that SEAs and LEAs become aware of the section 508 accessibility guides issued by the General Services Administration [GSA], which include not only specifications for products but extensive technical assistance as well.

COED Recommendation #48: The Congress should support new and existing assistive devices resource centers to provide information and instruction on the latest technological advances for persons who are deaf.

Status: Accomplished

PL 100-407, the Technology-Related Assistance for Individuals with Disabilities Act of 1988, signed by President Reagan on August 19, implemented this recommendation by authorizing grants to support information and referral programs and technical assistance projects, including assistive devices resource centers. Public information services and training programs for educators, counselors and others are an integral part of TRAIDA. The national technical assistance to States project authorized by title I was awarded to RESNA, an interdisciplinary association for the advancement of rehabilitation and assistive technology, headquartered in Washington, DC.

Meanwhile, the Department of Education awarded grants to Gallaudet and to the University of Delaware to demonstrate how new technology can help deaf people.

Unmet Needs: The Department of Education should ensure that TRAIDA grant recipients place priority on provision of assistance to deaf and hearing-impaired persons, who have great potential to benefit from existing and emerging technologies.

COED Recommendation #49: The Department of Education should support national symposia on media and technology to provide information on the most recent advances in applied technology for individuals who are deaf.

Status: Significantly Accomplished

In 1991, OSEP proposed numerous technology projects featuring symposia and other dissemination strategies. In fact, most of OSERS' recent grants, contracts, and cooperative agreements for technology projects feature outreach and dissemination activities, including symposia. The Department plans to bring together local news captioners by September, 1991, to offer suggestions for improving quality. [Some local stations use TelePrompter text as captions, leaving many videotape segments of news broadcasts uncaptioned. While inexpensive, this approach certainly can be improved with advanced technology.]

Another symposium, planned by the National Technical Institute for the Deaf, the Conferences of Educational Administrators Serving the Deaf, and other organizations in response to COED Recommendation #49, will take place in May, 1992, in Rochester, New York. This National Symposium on Educational Applications of Technology for Deaf Students is designed to acquaint educators and deaf adults with emerging technologies.

Unmet Needs: None, other than continuation of current practices of requiring research projects to place more emphasis on dissemination, including symposia.

Captioned Films

COED Recommendation #50: The Department of Education should implement the following administrative improvements in the Media Services and Captioned Films program: lessen the gap between costs incurred and reimbursements, continue to make more prints available to depositories, increase the number of new titles distributed yearly, provide more information to schools about the program, continue to eliminate old films and upgrade others, shorten the time required for distribution, and investigate the use of current technology to enhance the captioning of films and media.

Status: Accomplished

The Will letter[10] to Senator Harkin of June 16, 1988 stated that computers were being used to speed up manufacturing of captioned negatives and video masters. Some 500 titles were to be transferred from 16mm film to VHS videotape in 1988, she said.

Dr. Davila's September 25, 1989 letter[4] added that 116 additional educational titles were captioned during Fiscal Year [FY] 1988, with another 99 to be captioned in FY 1989 and 100 in FY 1990. [The actual FY 1990 total was 98.] He said that older films were regularly being eliminated from the program, as COED recommended, and that investigations of current technologies were an ongoing part of the program.

PL 101-476, the EHA Amendments of 1990, added "hard of hearing" to "deaf" and added a priority to use captioning to help eradicate illiteracy among persons with disabilities. The Department responded with FY 1991 projects in these areas.

Unmet Needs: Expanding services to hard of hearing persons may be accomplished, in part, by means of an agreement between the Department and Self Help for Hard of Hearing People [SHHH]. This rapidly growing, international network of local chapters is the single most vigorous service delivery system now available to reach hard of hearing youth and adults. The chapters' monthly meetings are logical settings for captioned films to be screened.

References

[33]Bowe, F. (1989) Prospects for Built-in Television Captioning by Japanese and Korean Manufacturers. Unpublished report prepared for World Rehabilitation Fund, October 2. The WRF's support enabled the author to respond to Senator Harkin's request. [Copies: Department of Counseling, Research, Special Education and Rehabilitation, Hofstra University, Hempstead, NY 11550; 516-463-5782 (v) or -5153 (TDD).]

[34]Huber, B. A. (1990) Testimony before the Communications Subcommittee, U. S. Senate, June 20. Mr. Huber was vice president, marketing for Zenith, the only U.S.-owned TV manufacturer. [Copies: Communications Subcommittee, Hart 227, U. S. Senate, Washington, DC 20510.]

[35]Shapiro, G. J. (1990) Letter to Senators Harkin and Inouye, July 20. [Copies: EIA, 2001 I Street NW, Washington, DC 20006.]

[36]House Report 101-172, Departments of Labor, Health and Human Services, and Education and Related Agencies Appropriations Bill, FY 1990, June 25, 1989, p. 148 on decoders.

[37]Ferguson, R. (1990) "Law May Soon Ease Access to Captioned TV for Deaf." *Wall Street Journal*, August 22, pp. B1, B4.

[38]Foerstel, K. (1989) "Hearing-Impaired Aided in Following Meetings." *Roll Call*, October 30, p. 20.

Chapter 8

Other Recommendations

Other Recommendations

Summary

The Commission's final two recommendations responded to Congress's request for guidance on clearinghouses and suggested that a study group similar to ours address the special concerns of deaf-blind individuals.

Clearinghouses

COED Recommendation #51: The Congress should require the Department of Education to strengthen public awareness of its clearinghouses by providing toll-free access to the best of these services and by funding captioned public service announcements.

Status: Significantly Accomplished

PL 100-407, the Technology-Related Assistance for Individuals with Disabilities Act of 1988, authorizes extensive public awareness activities about technologies helping persons with disabilities, including deaf people. It also requires the Secretary of Education to study the feasibility of a national information and program referral network; the report of that study is likely to be released in Spring, 1991.

PL 100-553, the National Deafness and Other Communication Disorders Act of 1988, requires the National Institute on Deafness and Other Communication Disorders [NIDCD] to "establish a[n] . . . Information Clearinghouse to facilitate and enhance, through the effective dissemination of information, knowledge and understanding of disorders of hearing and other communication processes by health professionals, patients, industry and the public." [Section 464B(b).] In January, 1989, a 200-member task force developed for NIDCD a Research Plan, which included recommendations for the clearinghouse. In October, 1989, NIDCD hosted a meeting specifically about the clearinghouse.

The Department of Education supports a National Information Center for Children and Youth with Handicaps, the HEATH Resource Center at the American Council on Education in Washington, and a Parent Information Center in New Hampshire.

PL 101-476, the EHA Amendments of 1990, require in section 622(d) that the Department of Education support a national clearinghouse on deaf-blindness. This is to include maintaining a computerized database on local, regional and national resources.

Unmet Needs: The Commission sensed in 1987 that there already were too many clearinghouses. The need now is coordinate these and to publicize them more widely.

Deaf-Blindness

COED Recommendation #52: The Department of Education should establish a Committee on Deaf/Blindness to make a study of the needs of persons who are deaf and blind and to make a report of its findings and recommendations.

Status: Significantly Accomplished

The Commission's Members did not feel qualified to assess the state-of-the-art in education of deaf-blind persons. We requested, and received, an excellent report on that topic from Art Roehrig. His report supported our contention that the issues were important and complex enough to deserve study on their own.

The Will June 16, 1988 letter[10] to Senator Harkin said it was "not advisable to create a special Committee on Deaf-Blindness." Dr. Davila's September 25, 1989 letter[4], however, said: "We will explore the possibility" of such a Committee. In 1990, OSERS created a working group comprised of staff members from RSA, OSEP and NIDRR to study how COED Recommendation #52 could be implemented. As a result of that effort, a symposium on deaf-blindness issues was scheduled for early summer 1991.

Unmet Needs: As noted above, PL 101-476 requires the Department of Education establish a national clearinghouse on deaf-blindness. It also explains that services for deaf-blind persons are to include early intervention services for infants and toddlers. The EHA Amendments also remove the age 22 minimum for individuals receiving services under section 622 in order to facilitate transition from school to adulthood, and authorize independent living and competitive employment as permitted activities funded under that section. These steps must now be taken. In addition, the Department should take seriously the recommmendations emerging from the summer 1991 symposium on deaf-blindness. Finally, the Department from time to time has asked Congress for permission to merge funds earmarked for programs serving deaf-blind persons with other funds designated for "severely disabled" individuals. The Commission disagreed with that idea. The deaf-blind population has so many severe needs, and is so vulnerable to pressure from larger, less severely communication-disabled groups, that funds to serve its members must remain discrete and readily identifiable.

Where Do We Go From Here?

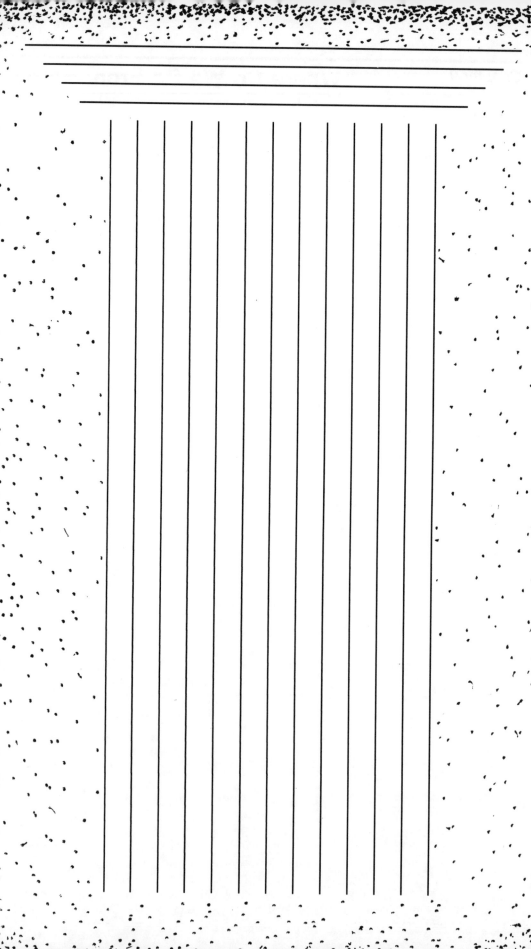

Where Do We Go From Here?

Summary

Three years after publication of *Toward Equality*, Congress and the Executive Branch have made very considerable progress toward the goals established by the Commission on Education of the Deaf.

As remarkable as this rapid progress is, most of it has taken place at the national policy level. America is a very large country, very diversified in resources and needs. It is too much to expect that in three short years policy changes at the Federal level would lead to "real life", grass roots improvements in the quality of life for the average deaf American.

That now is our most important goal—to translate policy improvements in Washington to concrete enhancements in programs and services beyond the Beltway. It is sometimes said of Washington that the city is 30 square miles surrounded by reality. There is much truth to this joking put-down of the Nation's Capital. We must never lose sight of the fact that laws, regulations and court decisions must be implemented in such places as Des Moines, Iowa; Wausau, Wisconsin; Brooklyn, New York; Carbondale, Illinois; and Portland, Oregon. Until the lives of deaf Americans in these and many thousands of other cities and towns are more equitable, we can only say we are still "approaching" equality—we are not done yet.

Prevention and Early Intervention

It is important that Congressional authorizing and appropriations committees send an unmistakable message to the National Institute on Deafness and Other Communication Disorders [NIDCD] that its first name is "Deafness". The intent of the chief sponsors, the late Claude Pepper [D-FL] in the House and Senator Harkin in the Senate, was to elevate research attention to deafness and hearing loss. NIDCD leaders to date have given insufficient attention to such issues as visual information processing, acquisition of sign language, and language learning—and they have failed to bring into the Institute deaf leaders with the vision to guide NIDCD toward a future that makes a difference for deaf people.

In the area of early intervention, it is vital for advocates to note that Part H of IDEA does not contain a "least restrictive environment" requirement. The conflict in Part B between "where" children are served and "what" and "how" they are helped does not constrain progress under Part H. Thus, individual and family services offered to infants and toddlers aged birth to two years inclusive may be provided in any suitable setting—including personal instruction at home and intensive deaf-children-only programs at center schools. Everything we know about deafness and language tells us that early intervention is a *sine qua non* for deaf children to acquire mastery of language.

We have a very severe shortage of early intervention personnel trained to work with deaf infants, toddlers and preschoolers. IDEA now provides priorities in personnel preparation and student financial assistance, with first priority reserved for disabled (in this case, deaf) and minority-group candidates.

Elementary and Secondary Education

This report demonstrates that the lowest level of implementation of all of COED's 52 recommendations is found in elementary and secondary education, with only one out of 14 recommendations rated "significantly accomplished" or better. There can be little doubt that for further progress to occur in deafness education, the emphasis must be placed upon improving the quality of preschool, elementary and secondary programming.

As frustrating as it is for advocates to make progress under the Individuals with Disabilities Education Act [IDEA], positive action *is* possible. The letters from Lawrence Siegel, of California, and Robert Dawson, of Florida, illustrate the most efficacious approach. Both wrote to the US Department of Education, highlighting very specific areas in which policy interpretation was requested. These letters gave the Department an opportunity to write *policy letters*[8,13] directly on the issues affecting deaf and other children with communication-related special needs. In this way, the Department was able to move forward in deafness without at the same time risking a move backwards with respect to other disability categories. It is vital that advocates highlight for the Department the specific, case-by-case, individual needs of deaf children in letters to ED so that policy-letter responses may give us further progress.

The time has come to move from "equity" (guaranteeing every child with a disability access to an education from which he or she can "benefit") to "excellence".[39,40] The Department of Education already has the authority to recognize, and provide awards to, outstanding programs nationwide. The much-publicized Malcolm Baldrige National Quality Awards for business offer a model for what ED could do in special education. Congress can go further—and should.

The Federal Government directly funds two "model" schools—the Kendall Demonstration Elementary School [KDES] and the Model Secondary School for the Deaf [MSSD]—and thus can instruct these schools to respond to national priorities in deafness education. Both are authorized under title I of the Education of the Deaf Act [EDA], which is up for reauthorization by mid-1992. It is important for Congress to take full advantage of this reauthorization process to establish at KDES and MSSD the kinds of program standards needed by special educators nationwide as guidance for how they can move toward excellence in deafness education.

Assuming that EDA directs KDES and MSSD to develop and demonstrate program standards, it would be appropriate for Congress in 1994 or 1995, when reauthorizing IDEA, to direct the US Department of Education to provide guidance to States with respect to adopting similar program standards. Much of the lack of action by the Department on COED Recommendations #3-16 and #29-39 can be traced to the belief by Department lawyers that ED lacks Congressional authority to tell the States what to do. Such passivity is increasingly irresponsible on the Department's part, given the dismal performance of SEAs and LEAs in educating deaf children and youth.

There is a very severe shortage of deaf, ASL-fluent personnel in the public schools, especially at the preschool and elementary levels. IDEA now allows the Department of Education to provide first priority in student financial assistance to disabled (in this case, deaf) and minority-group candidates. More funding for personnel preparation is important. The *Twelfth Annual Report to Congress*[20] revealed that, as of the 1987–1988 school year, the States reported needing 610 additional special education teachers for deaf children, yet ED's Department of Personnel Preparation funded that year only 115 graduates of deafness education programs nationwide.

The Department of Education has gone as far as it can under existing law to recognize American Sign Language as a "native language". Congress will have to do the rest. EDA offers an opportunity to amend IDEA section 602(a)(21) by striking "has" and adding after "native language" the following: "means American Sign Language and". Alternatively, Congress could amend section 7003(a)(2) of the Bilingual Education Act when it comes up for reauthorization in 1992 to accomplish the same purpose. That, however, is politically unlikely. As a third option, Congress could amend section 602(a)(21) of IDEA when IDEA is reauthorized.

Briefly, it is time in deafness education to look more at "what" and "how" deaf children are taught, and less at "where".[39,40]

Postsecondary Education

The single highest priority in this category is implementation of COED Recommendation #20. Two one-year demonstration projects are showing how non-college-bound deaf youth and adults may be helped to live productive, self-sufficient lives. The funding for these programs, in Seattle, Washington and Queens, New York, runs out in September, 1991. It is important for Congress when reauthorizing EDA to provide expanded funding for comprehensive rehabilitation centers for this population.

COED noted in *Toward Equality* that only a small minority of the 3,000-plus colleges and universities in the United States appear to be in full compliance with section 504 of the Rehabilitation Act of 1973. Fewer than 200 provide such support services as interpreters, readers, and notetakers for deaf students. The record of the US Department of Education's Office for Civil Rights [OCR] in investigating colleges and universities for section 504 violations is not an encouraging one. OCR must become much more aggressive about seeking full compliance.

The need for a fifth RPEPD in the Southwest region has been reaffirmed by the Research and Training Center on Deafness and Hearing Impairment at the

University of Arkansas.[25] It is logical that the four existing programs, and a fifth, be authorized in EDA rather than in IDEA. The authorization ceiling should be at least $5 million so as to maintain the existing four programs at current spending levels while providing for a fifth program.

Research

This report demonstrates progress in studying the difficult problems associated with language acquisition by deaf children and youth. Although more resources are being devoted to this issue, in response to COED's recommendations, we still have a long way to go before we understand how to teach English and ASL to deaf students so that they can consistently perform beyond the current third- to fourth-grade levels of reading achievement.

Professional Standards

Interpreter standards for both education and rehabilitation are lacking. ED at present relies almost exclusively upon private universities with which it has cooperative agreements or grants to advise States about professional standards for interpreters. It is important that the Department itself begin recommending such standards to State education and rehabilitation agencies.

It is important, too, that the Department tell SEAs and LEAs that they should insist on professional standards such as those proposed in *Toward Equality* for teachers, teacher aides, and related services personnel. The need is particularly urgent in public elementary and secondary schools serving deaf children placed in regular, resource, or special classrooms. Studies such as the ICD *Report Card* survey[15] reaffirmed COED's finding that special educators and related services personnel are less than adequately prepared to work with deaf and disabled students.

Technology

The Americans with Disabilities Act, title IV, allows for improved technology to be used to provide full and equal access to the nation's telecommunications networks for deaf, hearing-impaired and speech-impaired persons. At least in theory, placement of computer speech recognition systems into the telecommunications network could enable a deaf student to use an inexpensive, "dumb" terminal on a school desk to read what teachers and other students say in class— and to use a similar low-cost terminal to understand what is said on the telephone. Such speech recognition systems could also, at least in theory, obviate the need to encode captions for television. And they could even provide access, for the first time ever, to radio.

As tantalizing as these visions are, they require that deaf people be able to read— and read well. Once again, the greatest need in deafness education is to teach language skills. We have commercial products costing under $100 which proof-read text—essays written for teachers, articles prepared for school newspapers—and highlight grammar, syntax and spelling errors. These software programs do not yet recognize and help correct "deaf English". That will come, however, with time. It will help deaf children and youth tremendously to be able to see their own errors and correct them instantly. In time, we might even see such programs used on TDDs, dumb terminals and PCs to allow deaf persons to produce error-free English text on telephone calls.

Some time after the Year 2000, fiber-optic cable will reach into most American homes. Fiber optics can "switch" both voice and video. Thus, it might become possible for deaf persons with very limited English skills to "talk" on the telephone with any other American using a TV-phone-like device.

Research and development stimulating such advances clearly are important. Just as important, however, is finding ways to make these products, when they become commercially feasible, affordable to deaf people. We need to study ways to move away from "intelligent" terminals which cost in the thousands of dollars and toward "intelligent" networks which do the expensive translations so as to allow deaf people to use under-$100 dumb terminals.

All of this suggests that Congress carefully examine the possibility of using the 1934 Communications Act as a vehicle for placing into America's multi-billion-dollar telecommunications network the speech recognition, speech synthesis, and grammar-correcting capabilities needed by many deaf people.

Other

More than a generation passed between the "Babbidge Report" of 1965 and the COED Report of 1988. It is important that we provide for a follow-up study assessing progress on COED's recommendations far more quickly than we did on the Babbidge recommendations. Congress has the opportunity in title III of EDA to authorize a follow-along study commission in 1996. That would ensure that findings and recommendations are available to Congress when it reauthorizes EDA in 1997.

References

[39]DuBow, S. (1989) "Into the Turbulent Mainstream—A Legal Perspective on the Weight to be Given to the Least Restrictive Environment in Placement Decisions for Deaf Children." *Journal of Law and Education*, 18, 2, 215–228.

[40]Silverstein, R. (1986) "The Legal Necessity for Residential Schools Serving Deaf, Blind, and Multi-handicapped Sensory-Impaired Children." *American Annals of the Deaf*, 131, 80–84.

Recommendations

COED Recommendation

#1: The Congress should establish a National Institute on Deafness and Other Communication Disorders within the National Institutes of Health.

Significantly Accomplished

#2: The Department of Education, in collaboration with the Department of Health and Human Services, should issue federal guidelines to assist states in implementing improved screening procedures for each live birth. The guidelines should include the use of high-risk criteria and should delineate subsequent follow-up procedures for infants and young children considered to be at risk for hearing impairments.

Significantly Accomplished

#3: The Congress and the Department of Education should ensure that facilitating English language acquisition in students who are deaf (including vocal, visual, and written language) is a paramount concern guiding the implementation of exemplary practices; the establishment of program models; the dissemination of research priorities; the design of curricula, materials, and assessment instruments; and the provision of professional and parent training. Language acquisition should be a top priority in federally funded research.

Significantly Accomplished

#4: The Department of Education should provide guidelines and technical assistance to state and local educational agencies and parents to ensure that an individual education program for a child who is deaf takes into consideration the following: severity of hearing loss and the potential for using residual hearing; academic level and learning style; communicative needs and the preferred mode of communication; linguistic, cultural, social, and emotional needs; placement preference; individual motivation; and family support.

Partly Accomplished

#5: The Department of Education should refocus the least restrictive environment concept by emphasizing appropriateness over least restrictive environment.

Partly Accomplished

#6: The Department of Education should issue a policy statement to permit consideration in placement decisions of curriculum content and methods of curricular delivery required by the nature or severity of the child's handicapping conditions.

Partly Accomplished

#7: The Department of Education should issue guidelines and standards by which school officials and parents can, in selecting the least restrictive environment, consider potential

Partly Accomplished

COED Recommendation	*Status*

harmful effects on the child or on the quality of services which the child needs.

#8: The Department of Education should publish in the *Federal Register* a policy interpretation that removal from the regular classroom does not require compelling evidence.

No Action

#9: The Department of Education should monitor states to ensure that they maintain and nurture center schools as placement options as required by law.

Partly Accomplished

#10: The Department of Education should monitor states to ensure the availability and appropriateness of integrative programs for students in center schools.

Partly Accomplished

#11: The Department of Education should issue a policy statement requiring that school personnel inform parents of all options in the continuum of alternative placements during each individualized education program conference.

Partly Accomplished

#12: The Department of Education should monitor states to ensure that the evaluation and assessment of children who are deaf be conducted by professionals knowledgeable about their unique needs and able to communicate effectively in the child's primary mode of communication.

Partly Accomplished

#13: The Department of Education should encourage states to establish program standards for deaf students requiring special schools or classes.

Partly Accomplished

#14: The Congress should pass a "Quality in Deaf Education" bill that would provide incentives to the states to enhance the quality of services provided to students who are deaf.

No Action

#15: The Department of Education should take positive action to encourage practices under the Bilingual Education Act that seek to enhance the quality of education received by limited-English-proficiency children whose native (primary) language is American Sign Language.

No Action

#16: The Congress should amend the Education of the Deaf Act to set certain priorities at the Kendall Demonstration Elementary School and the Model Secondary School for the Deaf, require annual reports to the Congress and the President, and require an evaluation and report every five years by the Department of Education's liaison office.

No Action

COED Recommendation   *Status*

#17: The Congress should increase funding to strengthen each Regional Postsecondary Education Program for the Deaf by providing a broader range of educational options, including vocational and technical training, 2-year junior college, and baccalaureate programs. The number of Regional Postsecondary Education Program for the Deaf should be increased to five. The additional program should be established in the southwest region of the United States to provide greater geographical coverage of the nation.

Significantly Accomplished

#18: A 5-year funding cycle should be established for the Regional Postsecondary Education Programs for the Deaf.

Accomplished

#19: The Congress should authorize funds for each Regional Postsecondary Education Program for the Deaf to provide adult and continuing education programs within their respective regions and to assist other local educational institutions in providing such programs to adults who are deaf.

Accomplished

#20: The Congress should establish one comprehensive service center in each of the ten federal regions of the United States. These centers may be located in existing facilities or may be stand-alone units. The Commission further recommends that the comprehensive service centers be funded through a competitive bid process.

Partly Accomplished

#21: The Congress should amend the Education of the Handicapped Act and the Education of the Deaf Act to direct the Department of Education's liaison office to: (1) coordinate the activities of Gallaudet University, the National Technical Institute for the Deaf, and the Regional Postsecondary Education Programs for the Deaf to ensure the quality of the programs and to avoid unnecessary duplication; (2) review and comment on workplans relating to research, demonstration and evaluation activities, technical assistance, and development of instructional materials; and (3) assist in the preparation of budget requests.

Accomplished

#22: The Department of Education should conduct program evaluations at Gallaudet University, the National Technical Institute for the Deaf, the Regional Postsecondary Education Programs for the Deaf, and the proposed comprehensive service centers on a 5-year cycle, and submit a report of its evaluation with recommendations, to the authorizing committees of the Congress. The evaluation team should consist of outside experts in the field of deafness, program evaluation, education, and rehabilitation, including persons who are deaf.

Partly Accomplished

COED Recommendation   *Status*

#23: The National Technical Institute for the Deaf should be   **Accomplished**
permitted to admit foreign students who are deaf. However,
the number of foreign students should be limited to 10 percent
of the student body at Gallaudet University and the National
Technical Institute for the Deaf. Tuition should be increased
to foreign students to cover 75% of the average per student
costs at these two institutions.

#24: The Congress should deny Gallaudet the latitude to   **Accomplished**
accept hearing students to its baccalaureate programs.

#25: Gallaudet University, the National Technical Institute   **Significantly**
for the Deaf, and the Regional Postsecondary Education Pro-   **Accomplished**
grams for the Deaf should continue to strengthen the positive
efforts they have already made in recruiting, hiring, and promoting qualified applicants and employees who are deaf.

#26: The Congress should amend the Education of the Deaf   **Significantly**
Act to require that a majority of the members of the governing   **Accomplished**
and advisory bodies of Gallaudet University, the National
Technical Institute for the Deaf, and the Regional Postsecondary Education Programs for the Deaf be persons who are deaf.

#27: The Congress should establish a National Center on   **Obviated**
Deafness Research within Gallaudet University. Present fund-
ing at Gallaudet University for research-related purposes
would not necessarily be increased, but would be managed by
the Center. A significant portion of the Center's research
funds should be awarded competitively to other qualified
research organizations.

#28: The Congress should direct Gallaudet University and the   **Partly**
National Technical Institute for the Deaf to develop concrete   **Accomplished**
research plans and to provide them for public comment by
consumers and researchers. The projects then should be
selected in conjunction with a program review process involving (principally) the best researchers in the field.

#29: The Department of Education should require state edu-   **Partly**
cational agencies to conduct statewide planning and imple-   **Accomplished**
mentation activities that specifically address the educational
and psychological needs of families with young children who
are deaf. Individuals working with young deaf children and
their families should be professionally trained in the area of
deafness and early intervention.

#30: The Department of Education should suggest that at   **Partly**
least one member appointed to each State Interagency Coordi-   **Accomplished**

COED Recommendation	*Status*

nating Council be knowledgeable about deafness.

#31: The Department of Education should ensure that grants for personnel training be targeted to personnel providing special services, preschool, and early intervention services to deaf children, from birth to age 5, and their families. Training should also be provided to adults who are deaf to prepare them to work as facilitating team members in local intervention programs.

Partly Accomplished

#32: The Department of Education should provide guidelines for states to include in their state plans such policies and procedures at least as stringent as those set by the Council on Education of the Deaf, to ensure that professionals in educational programs for students who are deaf are adequately prepared and trained.

Partly Accomplished

#33: The Department of Education should require states to ensure that persons employed to teach in special education programs demonstrate competence in the instructional practices and communication methods utilized within those programs.

No Action

#34: The Department of Education should require states to ensure that regular classroom teachers serving students who are deaf in their classes receive the necessary technical assistance and training to meet the special educational needs of the students.

No Action

#35: The Congress should re-establish federal support for teacher preparation, including the recruitment of highly qualified applicants, in the field of education of the deaf. Priority for fellowships to qualified applicants should be awarded to members of minority groups and persons who are deaf.

Accomplished

#36: The Department of Education, in consultation with consumers, professionals, and organizations, should provide guidelines for states to include in their state plans such policies and procedures for the establishment and maintenance of standards to ensure that interpreters in educational settings are adequately prepared, trained, and evaluated.

Significantly Accomplished

#37: The Congress should provide funding to develop training programs, design curricula, and award stipends to recruit and train potential and working educational interpreters.

Accomplished

#38: The Congress should fund section 315 of the Rehabilitation Act. The Department of Education should establish stan-

Partly Accomplished

dards for interpreters in the field of rehabilitation and other
human services settings.

#39: The Department of Education should provide an **Accomplished**
increased number of traineeships for trainees specializing in
deafness.

#40: The Congress should require the Federal Communica- **Obviated**
tions Commission to issue regulations as it deems necessary to
require that broadcasters and cable-TV programmers caption
their programming.

#41: The Congress should establish a Corporation of Closed **Obviated**
Captioning to coordinate the distribution of federal funds for
captioning projects. The Corporation would neither perform
captioning services, nor compete for funds with captioners.

#42: The Congress should require the Federal Communica- **Accomplished**
tions Commission to issue rules as it deems reasonable and
necessary to make new TV sets capable of decoding closed
captions. Until such TV sets become widely available, federal
funds for decoder development and manufacturing should be
made available to increase the distribution of existing
decoders, including provision of free decoders to persons who
are deaf.

#43: Federal proceedings and meetings should be communi- **Significantly**
catively accessible for people who are deaf through captioning, **Accomplished**
assistive listening devices, and interpreters (when needed and
arranged for in advance).

#44: Instructional materials financed and/or disseminated by **Significantly**
the federal government, including materials for public view- **Accomplished**
ing and employment training, should have open captions.

#45: The Congress should caption its own televised proceed- **Significantly**
ings, including House and Senate floor activity. **Accomplished**

#46: The Congress should provide funds for research, devel- **Accomplished**
opment, acquisition, and maintenance of technology to be
used for persons who are deaf.

#47: Federally funded school systems should specify accessi- **Significantly**
bility of electronic equipment to persons with disabilities when **Accomplished**
such equipment is procured, leased, or rented for faculty,
staff, or students.

#48: The Congress should support new and existing assistive **Accomplished**

devices resource centers to provide information and instruction on the latest technological advances for persons who are deaf.

#49: The Department of Education should support national symposia on media and technology to provide information on the most recent advances in applied technology for individuals who are deaf.

Significantly Accomplished

#50: The Department of Education should implement the following administrative improvements in the Media Services and Captioned Films program: lessen the gap between costs incurred and reimbursements, continue to make more prints available to depositories, increase the number of new titles distributed yearly, provide more information to schools about the program, continue to eliminate old films and upgrade others, shorten the time required for distribution, and investigate the use of current technology to enhance the captioning of films and media.

Accomplished

#51: The Congress should require the Department of Education to strengthen public awareness of its clearinghouses by providing toll-free access to the best of these services and by funding captioned public service announcements.

Significantly Accomplished

#52: The Department of Education should establish a Committee on Deaf/Blindness to make a study of the needs of persons who are deaf and blind and to make a report of its findings and recommendations.

Significantly Accomplished

P. L. 100-297, signed by President Reagan April 28, 1988.
29 USC 3281
The Bilingual Education Act of 1988 defines "limited English proficiency" and "native language" [sec. 7003]. The BEA reauthorization in 1992 offers the opportunity to include deaf individuals in these definitions.

P. L. 100-394, signed by President Reagan August 16, 1988.
47 USC 610
The Hearing Aid Compatibility Act of 1988 helped to implement COED Recommendation **#47** by making telephones in schools, workplaces, government offices, etc., more accessible to hard-of-hearing persons by requiring that they be hearing-aid compatible. See also, below.

P. L. 100-407, signed by President Reagan August 19, 1988.
29 USC 2201
The Technology Related Assistance for Individuals with Disabilities Act of 1988 implemented COED Recommendations **#46**, **#47**, and **#48** by providing federal funding for equipment accommodating the needs of deaf persons and others with disabilities, requiring states to acquire accessible equipment, and creating assistive device resource centers.

P. L. 100-542, signed by President Reagan October 28, 1988.
40 USC 762
The Telecommunications Accessibility Enhancement Act of 1988 implements COED Recommendation **#43** by establishing a federal TDD relay service enhancing access to federal offices, proceedings and meetings.

P. L. 100-553, signed by President Reagan October 28, 1988.
42 USC 201, 285
The National Deafness and Other Communication Disorders Act of 1988 implemented COED Recommendation **#1** by establishing a National Institute on Deafness and Other Communication Disorders (NIDCD) and **#51** on clearinghouses.

P. L. 101-336, signed by President Bush July 26, 1990.
42 USC 12101
The Americans with Disabilities Act of 1990 implemented COED Recommendations **#40**, **#43**, **#44** and **#45** by requiring captioning of federal and federally funded films and videos and accessibility of federal activities.

P. L. 101-431, signed by President Bush on October 16, 1990.
47 USC 609; 47 USC 303
The Television Decoder Circuitry Act of 1990 implemented COED Recommendation **#42** by requiring that all new 13" or larger TV sets sold or manufactured in the United States after July 1993 be equipped with built-in caption decoder chips.

P. L. 101-476, signed by President Bush on October 30, 1990.
20 USC 1400

The Education of the Handicapped Act Amendments of 1990 implemented COED Recommendations **#17** and **#19** by doubling the federal authorization ceiling for the Regional Postsecondary Education Programs for the Deaf [RPEPDs] and expanding their roles to include region-wide technical assistance services. It also implemented COED Recommendations **#31** on personnel training, **#35** on increasing the number of educators who are minority-group members and persons with disabilities, **#44** and **#51** by requiring captioning of video materials, and **#2** by emphasizing the importance of information dissemination to parents about early intervention. The Amendments changed the name of the basic law from "Education of the Handicapped Act" (popularly abbreviated to "EHA") to "Individuals with Disabilities Education Act" (IDEA).

Senate Resolution 101-13, January 25, 1990, amended the Senate rules allowing television broadcast of Senate proceedings. The amendment provided: "All coverage under this resolution shall be made available to hearing-impaired individuals via closed captions." In 1991, the Department of Education issued a request for proposals [RFP] to captioning vendors for the captioning of Senate broadcasts. Similar action in the House resulted in C-SPAN coverage of House "gavel-to-gavel" proceedings beginning February, 19, 1991. These resolutions implemented COED Recommendation **#45**.